Making Bentwood

Trellises Arbors Gates & Fences

Jim Long

Storey Publishing

The mission of Storey Publishing is to serve our customers by publishing practical information that encourages personal independence in harmony with the environment.

Edited by Deborah L. Balmuth
Cover design by Rob Johnson, Johnson Design
Front cover photograph © Charles Mann
Back cover photograph © Timothy Hursley
Text design and production by Mark Tomasi
Production assistance by Erin Lincourt
Photographs on pages 1, 2, 3, 8, 9, and 11 by Timothy Hursley; on pages 4, 5, 6, 7, 10, and 12 by Charles Mann
Line drawings by Rick Daskam
Copyright © 1998 by Jim Long

The information in this book is true and complete to the best of our knowledge. All recommendations are made without guarantee on the part of the author or Storey Publishing. The author and publisher disclaim any liability in connection with the use of this information. For additional information, please contact Storey Publishing, 210 MASS MoCA Way, North Adams, MA 01247.

Storey books are available for special premium and promotional uses and for customized editions. For further information, please call 1-800-793-9396.

Printed in China by Regent Publishing
20 19 18 17 16 15 14 13 12 11

Library of Congress Cataloging-in-Publication Data

Long, Jim, 1946 –
    Making bentwood trellises, arbors, gates & fences / Jim Long.
        p.   cm. — (Rustic home series)
    ISBN 1-58017-051-X (pbk.)
     1. Trellises—Design and construction—Amateurs' manuals. 2. Arbors— Design and construction—Amateurs' manuals.
     3. Fences— Design and construction—Amateurs' manuals. 4. Wood bending—Amateurs' manuals. I. Series.
TH4961.L66   1998
684.1'8—dc21   98-11781
                                                                   CIP

Contents

Introduction

My love for bentwood started in early childhood. I remember looking out the window of my bedroom as a small child, gazing on a winter landscape in which tree limbs bent in magical arches from the weight of the ice and snow.

In summer I daydreamed under an old apple tree, lying on my back, looking up at the bending limbs, heavy with a bounty of ripening fruit. I admired the natural curves of the weighted old limbs. I developed a strong attachment to those nature-formed shapes and to the architecture of wild things.

There was a kindly old neighbor who lived next door, just across the alley from my parents' yard. When Mrs. Oehring was out working in her yard or garden and saw me standing by the fence watching her, she would often invite me over. Sometimes she had fresh-baked bread sitting on the kitchen table and would butter a slice for me. She'd add a bit of her grape jam, made from the grapes on her arbor, then she'd set me on her knee and rock me in her old bentwood rocker and tell me stories.

Sometimes her stories were fun; sometimes she told them because she lived alone and just wanted someone to talk to. I would sit and rock with her, listening to her voice,

eating my jam and bread, and caressing the smooth willow arms of the antique rocker.

That ancient bent willow chair, with its corky bark and aged texture,

▼ Bentwood structures can divide a space or accent a meandering garden pathway.

fascinated me. I loved the idea of bending limbs into useful shapes, contouring them to forms that imitated nature and that could surround an old lady and a young child in comfort. The possibilities grew in my mind for bentwood.

My First Bentwood Projects

I began experimenting with bending woods when I was about 6 years old. I first tried using vines, shaping them into forms for various purposes. But vines had a mind of their own, I discovered, curving every which way and not easily conforming to my designs. They were more fragile than other woods and didn't last as long outside.

Next I started cutting small saplings, young trees that had sprung up from seeds dropped by birds or the wind. Those limber young seedlings grew along the garden fence and in the alley where I was allowed to play. I found that young elm saplings would bend well without breaking, and I began to make small objects for my mother's garden. I made primitive

▲ For the arch, use green, flexible wood that is sturdy enough to support the trellis and any vines or plants you want to display.

▲ The simple lines of bent wood bring an inviting natural order to our surroundings.

birdhouses, miniature log cabin—type structures with curved roofs and bentwood handles on top for hanging in trees. I made little trellises for Mother's gladiolus beds

(having gained greater respect for these plants as a result of a sorrowful lesson learned at age 5, when I pulled up the glads, bulbs and all, for a bouquet).

I experimented with peach limbs, which worked fairly well, although they were not as flexible for tight bends. Hickory worked very well, the young limbs being pliable and easily formed into my desired shapes.

Pecan, too, was easily found, along with cedar. Cedar lasts well outside but can be a bit sticky, and my mother, after seeing my stained hands and clothes, suggested, with an arched eyebrow, that I use other woods for my projects.

My parents taught me early on that the saplings I cut would come back again. I was not destroying the plant, simply harvesting a portion and leaving the root to grow again. In the small-town alleyway and fencerow where I gathered materials, I was actually helping keep the undergrowth in check.

Developing Simple Designs

As a child, I liked projects that were not complicated. My interest would wane if I started something too difficult, so I kept my designs simple. Trellises were my favorites, and I learned to use my tiny child-sized hammer and nails. My father let me use his pliers and some wire

▲ Each trellis is different and unique, defined by the wood chosen as much as the trellis maker's whims.

▲ Several naturally curled and bent vines enhance the rustic charm of this small trellis.

for the harder projects. Sometimes he would allow me to use his "real" tools, and I had more success with those.

Once I built a birdcage after seeing one in a woodcut print in an old book. I tried to imitate the curled Victorian designs, but mine looked more fragile, more rustic, and less Victorian. Not able to attract birds to the cage, I decided to put my favorite cat's kittens inside. At first they were content and played; then they grew frightened and began to plead to be let out. Seeing their terror at confinement, I soon let them free and discarded the birdcage. Perhaps that experience is why I still prefer my designs to be open and unrestrictive.

Practicing an Age-Old Craft

Years later, as an adult, I learned that the forms and styles of the bentwood furniture our neighbor owned dated back several centuries. Bentwood, particularly willow bentwood, enjoyed popularity in the United States in the early part of the twentieth century. It was also

closely related to the wicker furniture of the mid-1800s, made popular by Cyrus Wakefield. Wakefield's work was motivated by the enormous piles of rattan, a kind of climbing palm, that he found discarded on the wharves of Boston. Used on ships as dunnage to keep cargo from shifting, the rattan was going to waste once the ships

▲ The natural beauty of wood inspires and gives form to the limitless possibilities of bentwood construction.

▼ Here, two matching trellises are connected, making an eye-catching corner boundary for a small herb garden.

arrived in port. Inspired by wicker chairs that appeared in carvings and relief work from ancient Rome, Wakefield shaped the rattan into lavishly decorative furniture.

The Adirondack style of rustic furniture became popular in the nineteenth and early twentieth centuries. I had once mistakenly believed the Adirondack style to be the only

inspiration for later bentwood, but it was actually a revival of rustic furniture styles of earlier centuries.

The Timeless
Appeal of Bentwood

Rustic bentwood for the garden has come into and gone out of fashion over the years. There have been periods when people turned to making functional bentwood pieces for the home and garden out of necessity, when money or other materials were not available. The attraction of natural shapes also seems to increase during times of rapid industrial growth, when our more refined society has seemingly moved away from and lost touch with nature. Nature can bring a

▲ The smiling faces of sunflowers are as at home in a trellis as vines would be. This simple method keeps top-heavy plants from leaning into a garden pathway.

▲ Simple bent saplings of green wood make this arch practical for climbing beans.

feeling of serenity and order to an otherwise unnatural landscape, and the bending branches of wood seem to bring that natural order to people's surroundings. I feel certain (though there is little way to prove it) that the naturally curving shapes of laden fruit trees or the graceful curves of ice-covered limbs have inspired many cultures through the centuries to imitate those shapes in the home and garden.

Surely, native peoples must have used bent wood for training gourds and climbing vines. Surely, people in modern cultures were not the first to lie on their backs, staring up at the wondrous blue sky and floating clouds through arched tree branches, inspired to bend wood into natural shapes for permanent

▼ Green wood can be formed into intricate shapes that enhance a garden with timeless charm.

decorative pieces for their gardens. I am convinced that bentwood is as timeless as the garden itself, that people of any age and experience can appreciate the curving lines and intricate designs borrowed from nature and used in trellises, gates, fences, and arbors. Added to the garden, these structures tie us to the fertility of the ages, the hope for annual renewal and ever-bountiful harvests in our own backyards.

◀ Graceful arches of bent wood invite us to explore the garden beyond.

 # Selecting Wood

Bentwood projects, whether trellises, fences, arbors, gates, or others, can be made from a vast variety of woods. The main requirement is that you use green, flexible limbs for the arched parts of the trellis. The straight cross-pieces can be either green or dry wood, or a type that has less flexibility.

Some kinds of wood bend better than others, some are stronger, and some last longer outdoors. Wherever you live in North America, however, you will be able to locate some type of useful wood. (If finding appropriate green wood becomes too frustrating, see chapter 7 for some projects using other, dry materials.)

Determining What Type of Wood You Need

Before you begin searching for wood, it is helpful to have an idea about what wood qualities are required for your project. Do you want a small trellis to go in a patio planter left outdoors in the summer only, or do you plan to make a large trellis that will stay in the garden year-round? Will your trellis be placed near the house, under the eaves where weather seldom bothers, or will your trellis be beside the water garden where water is constantly splashing? Does your trellis serve only a decorative function, or will it be required to hold up considerable weight when the vines you plant are in full growth? Taking into account your particular needs will help you choose the best wood to use.

Wood Characteristics

The section beginning on page 16 describes the characteristics of the most common types of wood. The great part about making bentwood structures is that you are not trying to achieve a perfect, finished look. The unique curves and characteristics of the branches you select are part of the rustic charm.

Type and Size of Wood

The size of the wood needed depends on the finished size of the project. With trellises, project size can range from a miniature 10-inch-high planter piece that fits in a climbing ivy pot to 7- or 8-foot-high structures for your garden.

The wood that you select may be saplings, sprouts (sometimes called offshoots, meaning sprouts that come up around the trunk of a previously cut tree), or even curved lower limbs of larger trees. Native cedar, cypress, and some kinds of oak often have lower limbs that are naturally curved, and these can be used for trellises without damagng the tree. For a 7- or 8-foot trellis, you need wood that is about 1½ to 1¾ inches in diameter, or about the size of a cardboard roll inside paper towels. (The cardboard roll is a handy gauge to have with you when you cut your wood. If the large end of your longest piece fits comfortably inside the cardboard roll, then you have the right size.)

Since it is best to use green wood within 24 hours of cutting, you should wait until you have decided on a design (see chapter 3) and made a list of the arched pieces needed before you cut. For the straight crosspieces and non-bending decorative pieces, you can use green or dry wood.

Finding a Source for Wood

If you live in the country and have some acreage with timber, you probably already have all the materials you need for your projects. However, if you live in the suburbs, finding material requires more creativity. Here are some suggestions for finding the right wood.

- **Check out farms in the area.** Farmers often are willing to let you cut saplings from fencerows or from fields where young trees have invaded grazing areas. Find the owner, explain what you need, and ask for permission to cut (or ask for suggestions of other areas in case the answer is no). Also inquire about removing sprouts from the trunks of trees that have already been cut — this is wonderful, second-growth material, and there's little damage you can do as a novice to an old stump. (Don't be surprised if the farmer has a smirk on his face as you explain what you want.)

Cutting Responsibly

Always get permission from landowners if you plan to hunt for trellis material on land other than your own. If you are searching along roadsides or streams, check the laws in your area to be sure cutting on public land is allowed. And if you find wild areas where you can harvest materials, do it with regard to the environment: Leave some for others; don't destroy areas. Cut responsibly, as if it were your own land and you wanted your grandchildren to live there and build trellises, too.

How and When to Cut Limbs

Making bentwood structures is simple. Only a minimal number of tools is required. For gathering wood, I suggest a good sharp pair of loppers and a pair of pruners (see page 17 for full descriptions). You can make bentwood structures year-round, but you should harvest *only* the wood you need when you need it.

❧ **Call the utilities providers in your area.** Ask about obtaining limbs from areas where they might be cutting. Be forewarned that their insurance doesn't allow for you to be present while they are cutting down trees or doing other similar work, but they may know of areas where you could harvest limbs or saplings before they cut. You also may be able to gather downed limbs on their property.

❧ **Check the Yellow Pages for nurseries that do trimming and pruning for homeowners.** Stop by and visit with the manager of the trimming crew and explain what you are looking for. Often these folks will gladly sell freshly cut, green branches to avoid having to dispose of them. They may know of areas where they can cut what you want, or they may even steer you to an area where you can do the cutting yourself.

❧ **Check out vacant lots and alleys in your area.** Often cities will allow cutting in those areas. If the property is abandoned you can get permission to cut from the bank or city office responsible for the property. Alleys can be especially fertile ground for trellis material, and often shopkeepers are glad to have you clean out those areas — as long as you ask first.

Also check along drainage areas, city creeks, irrigation ditches, and other non-natural but weedy areas or man-made waterways. Willow, beech, birch, and other woods can be found there. Also look along railroad tracks, especially those abandoned and no longer used for trains. (Railroad traffic areas are usually sprayed to kill saplings, but when the tracks are abandoned, they can be a treasure trove of bentwood material.)

❧ **Check with the forestry service or conservation department in your area.** Sometimes certain areas are scheduled to be cleared, or you may be able to get a one-time permit to harvest saplings.

❧ **Call developers who own land that is scheduled for clearing.** Using saplings from these lots seems more ecologically sensible than having them wind up as fill under a shopping mall.

❧ **Use the trimmings from your own backyard.** Spring pruning of hedges, fruit trees, and other landscape trees can net you useful material.

❧ **Look for downed limbs after winter or summer storms.** Ask your neighbors for their limbs. They'll think you're nuts but will likely be glad to have you haul them away. Use caution, and avoid areas where there are downed electrical wires.

✿ **Grow your own.** If you have a bit of land and want a constant supply of useful material for bentwood projects, consider ordering willow cuttings (see Resources). Or you can plant cuttings or seedlings bought from nurseries. Even the conservation department in some states will sell you various kinds of seedlings for planting on your own land. Cutting some of these back encourages thicker regrowth, which is good for birds and other wildlife. In this way, you can manage your backyard for both wildlife and trellis making.

Working with Green Wood

Wood that is to be bent for trellises, gates, fences, arbors, and other similar structures should be freshly cut. Cut the wood no more than 24 hours before you begin the project. Some wood (red osier dogwood, weeping willow, and other varieties of willow) can be kept soaked for a few days after cutting, but the wood loses its flexibility quickly, and you will find that it breaks more easily than freshly cut green wood when bent.

Don't try to use dry wood for bentwood structures, except for the crosspieces and other straight pieces. No amount of resoaking of dry wood will give it back the flexibility it had when it was green. If you don't find enough wood to complete your planned project, work on it in stages, adding more wood as you find it.

Be aware that the wood will shrink naturally as the moisture leaves it, usually 25 percent or more in the first 10 days after it is cut. As the wood dries, it will lose its flexibility, so don't try to reshape the trellis once it is assembled. Joints that are wired will need to be retightened after shrinkage occurs.

Common Types of Wood

The following list will help you identify some of the common trees in your area and decide how suitable (or, in some cases, unsuitable) each is for making bentwood garden structures. You may want to get a good tree identification field guide to carry with you so that you can readily identify these trees by their leaves and bark.

Ash

(*Fraxinus* spp.)
Ash is a native species probably better known today as a landscape tree. Saplings found in alleyways, in fencerows near old homes, and in other urban locations make it useful as a trellis material.

Ash has a pleasant bark and texture, and it grows mostly straight with good proportions. All these characteristics lend themselves to project use. Varieties include red (*Fraxinus pennsylvanica*), pumpkin (*Fraxinus tomentosa*), water (*Fraxinus caroliniana*), blue (*Fraxinus quadrangulata*), white (*Fraxinus americana*), black (*Fraxinus nigra*), and green (*Fraxinus pennsylvanica*), among others. It has moderate durability — 2 to 3 years outdoors, longer if larger material is used — and retains most of its strength when dry.

- *Location:* Found in: Canada to Florida and west into the Mississippi Valley, Texas, and Oklahoma. Seedlings that have escaped from landscape plantings grow in alleys, fencerows, and vacant lots in cities and suburbs.

- *Disadvantage:* Not as flexible as some woods and may break if bent at sharp angles.

Aspen, Bigtooth
(*Populus grandidentata*)

Aspen, Quaking Aspen
(*Populus tremuloides*)

Both species are flexible and can be used for bentwood projects. They grow tall and straight with smooth bark. Like many trees that grow in areas of heavy snowfall, they must be flexible to bounce back from the weight of winter snows. The younger saplings and second-growth material are best.

- *Location:* Bigtooth aspen is found growing in dry soils and burned areas from Nova Scotia, Quebec, and Ontario south to Maryland, Virginia, North Carolina, Kentucky, and Tennessee. It also grows in northeast Iowa. Quaking aspen is found from Newfoundland and Labrador west to Alaska, and south to New Jersey, Virginia, West Virginia, and Ohio, as well as portions of Nebraska, Colorado, California, and the surrounding states. It has moderate durability, 3 to 4 years or longer.

- *Disadvantages:* Not as flexible when larger in diameter and may attract wood-eating insects. Easily

treated with wood preservative after it is dry, or it can be brought inside during the winter so that it will last longer.

Bald Cypress
(*Taxodium distichum*)

A large deciduous tree, grown occasionally as a landscape tree but normally found in its natural state growing in or near water. The swamp-draining practices of the 1940s, 1950s, and 1960s, however, left diminished native cypress stands. Formerly used primarily for fences, gates, and greenhouse construction due to its strength and extreme resistance to rot. It remains one of the most durable woods for a trellis, gate, or arbor (8–10 years or longer), but unless it grows in your own backyard or you live near southern wetlands, you probably won't find it.

- *Location:* Formerly found growing in wetlands from southern New Jersey south to Florida and west to Texas, including Arkansas, southern Missouri, Tennessee, and Kentucky. It has been nearly eliminated from most of those areas today, however.

- *Disadvantages:* Hard to find. Sapling trunks also tend to be short and stocky.

Birch
(*Betula* spp.)

Birch, like many wetland trees, is flexible when small. But the young wood has little strength, so it is prone to breaking when dry. It also is attractive to several kinds of wood-eating insects. However, the limbs and young saplings are excellent for intricate bends and decorative pieces for trellises, especially for trellises that are protected in winter or are used in protected areas indoors. Durability is 1 to 3 years.

- **Location:** Birch trees are common throughout the upper portion of the United States. White birch *(Betula papyrifera)* is found in Alaska, Newfoundland, Labrador, New England, Pennsylvania, West Virginia, Ohio, northern Illinois, and the mountains of North Carolina. Often grown as a landscape tree in many other parts of the United States along with European white birch *(Betula pendula),* which has naturalized in some areas.

  Copper, or river, birch *(Betula nigra)* is found along streams and wetlands in southern New Hampshire, New York, Indiana, Minnesota, and Kansas, as well as south to Florida and Texas. Other birch varieties are found in the Pacific Northwest, California, and the surrounding states.

- **Disadvantage:** Little strength to the dry wood when used outdoors and attractive to wood borers.

Cane, River

(Arundinaria gigantea)

This plant, along with cultivated bamboo, can be useful for trellis and arbor work. Both river cane and bamboo are quite flexible when newly cut and can be bent nearly double without breaking. The difficult part of using cane or bamboo is that it can't be nailed in the same way that twigs can. To make trellises, the material must be bound together or drilled through (with wire inserted in the holes); otherwise, it will split. Most cane and bamboo varieties last 4 to 8 years or longer outdoors, depending on the size of the material.

- **Location:** Canebrakes can be found in wetlands and along streams in the Mississippi Valley and in the South from Florida to Texas. Bamboo may escape cultivation and can be found from the Pacific states and British Columbia eastward, and in some southern states.

- **Disadvantage:** Must be bound or drilled rather than nailed.

Cedar, Native Red

(Juniperus virginiana)

This is a timber tree, often considered a weed tree by farmers because it encroaches on untilled fields. It is used for fence posts and for making cedar chests and lining closets, due to its ability to repel clothes moths. Cedar also is used for furniture and bowls, as the maroon-and-white wood is unusual and attractive. Durability is excellent, 6 to 8 years or longer.

Almost any shrub or tree in the juniper family has similar durability (even the overgrown junipers in the home landscape). When found growing close together in thickets, native cedar saplings tend to be very tall and slender with few limbs. Consistent in size from the base upward for several feet, they are very flexible. Native red cedar is one of the best trellis materials both for flexibility and for durability outdoors. It will last 6 to 8 years or longer.

- **Location:** Native cedar grows on both sides of the Mississippi River, through Ohio, Indiana, Tennessee, Kentucky, Missouri, Arkansas, Kansas, Oklahoma, Texas, and the surrounding states. Related varieties grow in the Northeast as well as in the South.

- **Disadvantages:** The sap can be slightly sticky, and the needles can be mildly irritating. It's best to wear gloves when working with cedar.

Cottonwood, Common

(Populus deltoides)

Similar to aspen, cottonwood has a more southern range. It is often used in landscaping and in shelter belts for wind protection. Its quick growth pattern is perfect for woodlots. Cottonwood is moderately useful. Durability is 1 to 3 years.

- **Location:** The common cottonwood is found in New Hampshire west to southern Saskatchewan and south to northwest Florida, central Texas, and western Kansas. Swamp cottonwood *(Populus heterophylla)* can be found from Connecticut and southeast Pennsylvania south to Florida and Louisiana and west to the Mississippi Valley, Ohio, Michigan, and Missouri. Balsam cottonwood *(Populus balsamifera)* is found in bottomlands from Alaska to British Columbia, Idaho, Nebraska, Colorado, Minnesota, New York, and Maine.

- **Disadvantages:** Will break if bent sharply. May last only 2 to 3 years outdoors.

Dogwood

(Cornus spp.)

Widely used as a landscape tree, dogwood is native to the central and eastern United States White dogwood *(Cornus florida)* is not useful for bentwood projects, except for very small desktop planter trellises, made from the second-growth sprouts of trees that have been cut. Red osier dogwood *(Cornus sericea)*, silky dogwood *(Cornus amomum)*, and rough-leaf dogwood *(Cornus drummondii)* are all desirable for small to medium-sized bentwood work, especially when cut and allowed to sprout back, such as along roadsides, under power lines, and in alleyways. The wood of these three is quite flexible (you can actually tie the whips into knots!) and will retain their reddish color when the trellis or piece has dried. Even wood the size of your thumb and 4 to 5 feet long will be flexible enough to bend into any shape you desire. Dogwood has moderate durability, 3 to 5 years.

- **Location:** Red osier is found in wet places in Newfoundland, Labrador, and Alaska south to the eastern and central United States. Silky dogwood grows in wetlands from Maine south to Georgia and Alabama and west into the Mississippi Valley. Rough-leaf dogwood occurs from Ontario south into Illinois, Nebraska, Oklahoma, Texas, and Mississippi.

- **Disadvantage:** As this is a large shrub rather than a tree, the only limitation is that the wood seldom grows beyond 5 or 6 feet, which will limit the size of the trellis. Dogwood is best used for small to medium-sized trellises.

Elder, Box

(Acer negundo)

The attractive green twigs make this a tempting wood to try, but the limbs are brittle and do not bend well. Box elder is not recommended except for portions of small trellises that are not bent. Durability is short, 1 to 2 years.

- **Location:** Found along riverbanks, in floodplains, and on fertile hillsides from Nova Scotia south to Florida and west to Texas and California.

- **Disadvantages:** Limbs are brittle and do not bend.

Elm

(Ulmus spp.)

Before the elm diseases of the 1950s and 1960s, American elm trees grew along the streets of many communities. The diseases wiped out many of those older trees, but many native elm species are still thriving, including winged elm *(Ulmus alata),* rock elm *(Ulmus thomasii),* and slippery elm *(Ulmus rubra),* among others. Any of these elms is useful for trellis projects due to the trees' excellent flexibility. The wood is not particularly strong, although it is preferable to birch or sycamore for bentwood projects. Elm has low to moderate durability, 1 to 4 years.

- **Location:** Bottomlands and rocky uplands from New England south to Florida and west to Kansas, Oklahoma, and Texas. Many varieties, including English elm *(Ulmus procera),* have been planted as landscape trees throughout the United States and have naturalized in areas where seed has spread.

- **Disadvantage:** Low to moderate durability outdoors.

Fruit Trees

Many varieties of fruit trees are useful for trellis making. Apple and pear trees both work well for small trellises. If you trim the trees regularly, you'll have a ready supply of wood for trellises. The smaller, flexible limbs of cherry trees work fairly well for planter-sized trellises, as do peach and apricot trimmings. Wild plum *(Prunus americana)* and cultivated plum varieties do not work well, as the limbs are not long and straight, and many varieties have thorns. They are not particularly flexible when bent into loops or trellis shapes. Fruit trees have poor durability, 1 to 3 years.

- **Location:** Fruit trees are found in home landscapes, backyards, and old orchards, with some escaping from cultivation (especially apple, peach, and cherry seedlings).

- **Disadvantages:** Useful only for small work due to the small limbs. Poor durability outdoors when dry (1–3 years).

Gum, Sweet

(Liquidambar styraciflua)

Sweet gum trees are stocky and not very useful for trellis work, with the exception of trees cut and allowed to sprout again. The young sprouts can be used with some success for small projects. Durability is poor, 1 to 3 years.

- **Location:** Wetlands across the Mississippi Valley east to New York and south to central Florida; also, in areas where they have naturalized from landscape plantings.

- **Disadvantage:** Not recommended for bending due to stockiness and bulk, but can be used for straight pieces. Sprouts can, however, be used for small trellises.

Hickory

(Carya spp.)

Saplings are very flexible and easy to work with. The bark is smooth and pleasant on the hands, and the saplings are well proportioned from base to tip. They do not grow as straight as cedar or birch, but nice little jogs in the wood add appeal to the finished piece. Hickory is highly recommended due to its flexibility, even though durability is moderate, 3 to 5 years (shorter for small pieces, longer for larger).

- **Location:** Found with other hardwood species such as oak and walnut across the central portion of the United States. Various species can be found from Quebec and Ontario south to Florida and Texas, up the Mississippi Valley, and in the surrounding areas.

- **Disadvantages:** Moderate durability and may be prone to some insect damage. However, clear wood preservative applied in the fall after the vining plants have died will preserve the trellis for several years.

Locust, Black

(Robinia pseudoacacia)
This is a small tree with a profusion of flowers in the spring. The wood is moderately useful for trellises. Some varieties of locust are said to be long-lasting when used as fence posts. Durability is moderate, 3 to 5 years, depending on the size used.

- **Location:** Grows from Canada south to Georgia and Louisiana and west to Oklahoma. Plantings in other areas of the country may have spread by seed and become naturalized. The trees are grown as windbreaks and wildlife cover in some areas.

- **Disadvantage:** Limited availability.

Locust, Honey

(Gleditsia triacanthos)
Young saplings are attractive (white-striped) and interesting in spite of very sharp thorns. For small planter-sized projects, the wood can be used after clipping off the young thorns. It will keep its nice color and texture after it dries. Sharp bends are usually not possible, although I have harvested the wood in early spring just before the leaves are about to emerge and have been able to make sharp bends by choosing the more flexible pieces. Durability is poor to moderate, 1 to 3 years, possibly longer.

- **Location:** Fields and woods from Ontario, Michigan, and South Dakota south to Florida, Texas, and Oklahoma.

- **Disadvantages:** Not especially flexible beyond sprouts up to 24 to 30 inches long. The thorns must be removed with pruners.

Maple

(Acer spp.)
Maple species are widely used as landscape trees in suburbs and cities. Some varieties, such as the silver maple *(Acer saccharinum)*, grow quickly into shade trees. Others, such as the sugar maple *(Acer saccharum)* are valued for their fall color (and for maple syrup in the northeastern states, where they are native).

None is particularly useful for bentwood projects, although young saplings of sugar maple, black maple *(Acer nigrum)*, red maple *(Acer rubrum)*, and striped maple, or moosewood *(Acer pensylvanicum)* should all be tried, as there is some variability in flexibility under different conditions. Generally, they break easily, but for small projects that require minimal bends, they can be useful.

Maples have poor to moderate durability, 1 to 3 years, possibly longer depending on the variety.

- *Location:* Maple varieties, both native and cultivated in landscape settings, can be found throughout the United States.

- *Disadvantages:* Some varieties break easily when bent but they can be used for limited projects, and it's well worth trying the types you have available.

Mulberry

(*Morus* spp.)
The two most prevalent species are red (*Morus rubra*) and white (*Morus alba*). Both the saplings and second-growth sprouts of these two trees are moderately useful for small trellis work. Durability is poor to moderate, 1 to 3 years.

- *Location:* Thickets and woods, as well as in alleys and vacant lots. Often planted to attract birds and are spread by seed. Found from New England south to Florida and west to Texas, Oklahoma, and beyond.

- *Disadvantage:* Will break if bent too sharply.

Nut Trees

Nut trees related to hickory include pecan (*Carya* spp.), black walnut (*Juglans nigra*), and butternut (*Juglans cinerea*). These can be used but are not as flexible as hickory. Young (2- to 3-year-old) pecan seedlings are the best option for bentwood. Black walnut and butternut are less useful but certainly can be tried if available.

- *Location:* Native and cultivated varieties of all three nut trees can be found throughout the United States. Pecans grow naturally along the Osage, Missouri, and Mississippi Rivers, as well as along rivers and steams in Oklahoma, Texas, and Georgia, and the surrounding regions. Black walnut is found in poorer soils on hillsides and in fields from Ontario, Minnesota, and South Dakota south to Oklahoma, Texas, and Florida. Butternut is found in fertile woods in New Brunswick and southeast Minnesota, south to South Carolina, Georgia, and Mississippi, and in rocky woods and along streams in Arkansas and Missouri. Durability is low to moderate, 1 to 3 years, depending on size.

- *Disadvantages:* Pecan, black walnut, and butternut are not very flexible, breaking if bent sharply. Saplings are not easily found unless you have access to timberland, and they tend to be short and stocky. They are best used as straight structural pieces.

Oak

(*Quercus* spp.)
Oak saplings, especially when growing close together, are flexible, straight, and usually easy to bend. The wood is strong, and durability is moderate to excellent, 3 to 8 years. Once made into a bentwood project, oak will last for several years outside.

- *Location:* There are several dozen varieties of oak, and one variety or another can be found anywhere in the United States. It isn't necessary to know exactly which oak you are working with, but identifying the variety by consulting a guidebook or asking for help from the local forestry or conservation service may make your project more interesting.

- *Disadvantages:* Oak saplings tend to be large at the bottom and stocky, even on relatively small (5- to 6-foot) seedlings, which makes them hard to bend. Limbs from larger trees can be used to good advantage.

Osage Orange

(Maclura pomifera)

This is a tough, extremely durable wood. Fence posts 6 inches in diameter are claimed to last 40 years or more, as the wood is resistant to rot and insects. Once the wood is cut and dried, it is so dense that it is almost impossible to cut.

Young saplings, as well as second-growth cuttings (small trees cut and allowed to sprout again), are flexible enough for bentwood projects. Durability is excellent, 6 to 10 years or longer.

- **Location:** Native to the United States; the Ozarks region of Missouri and Arkansas is said to have been named for it. (Ozarks is believed to have come from the French *bois d'arc,* taken from an earlier French

Osage Orange Hedges

Settlers moving west in the early 1800s took Osage orange cuttings with them. They planted the cuttings in Ohio, Indiana, Illinois, Iowa, Missouri, Kansas, and the surrounding region to form impenetrable hedges to keep livestock in pastures.

The trees were planted in rows spaced every 3 feet, then allowed to grow together into a dense hedge that was cut every 3 or 4 years. It was impossible for cattle or people to penetrate an Osage orange hedge due to the tough, dense limbs and the short thorns along them.

pronunciation of a Native American word for "bowed wood," meaning the wood used to make hunting bows. In Texas this tree is still called "bodark.") Found in thickets from New England south to Georgia, Texas, and the Mississippi Valley, Osage orange also grows in some areas of Washington and Oregon.

Osage orange is a tough, durable wood that will last for 6 to 10 years outdoors.

- **Disadvantage:** Short thorns along the limbs of young saplings, although they are easily removed with pruners.

Privet, Common

(Ligustrum vulgare)

Privet California

(Ligustrum ovalifolium)

The common privet is a tall shrub (10–20 feet) of European origin used for hedges around lawns and gardens. Repeated pruning encourages denser growth that is flexible for small to medium-sized trellises. Larger limbs from mature shrubs can yield structural pieces for even large trellises. Both varieties have escaped cultivation and are similarly useful. Privet wood trellises are moderately durable, 3 to 5 years outdoors. The privet is useful for a living arbor (see page 91).

- **Location:** Privet can be found naturalized along the edges of woods, in alleys and abandoned lots, and on roadsides throughout much of the United States.

- **Disadvantage:** Generally useful only for small trellises, although larger limbs found on mature shrubs can be used for larger projects.

Redbud

(Cercis canadensis)

This American native, ornamental tree is widely planted for its early-spring profusion of startling purple-pink flowers. The young sprouts of trees that have been cut back are moderately flexible and can be useful in small to medium-sized projects. Saplings or sprouted limbs up to the size of your little finger are flexible and can be bent without breaking. Durability is 1 to 3 years.

- *Location:* Woodlands from Canada, New York, Wisconsin, and Nebraska south to Florida and Texas, as well as throughout the Mississippi Valley.

- *Disadvantage:* Good for moderate bends but may break if bent sharply.

Sassafras

(Sassafras albidum)

This very fragrant wood is known for the tea made from the roots after the bark is removed. Once sought as a lightweight, very strong wood for making boat oars, today this native American tree is mostly ignored. Occasionally, you will find sassafras used as a landscape tree because of the brightly colored orange, red, and yellow foliage in the fall.

Young saplings are green at the tips, tapering to corky, smooth bark below, and are easily cut. The wood is useful for crosspieces and straight pieces in latticework, but it will break easily if bent sharply. I often use this wood for everything except the actual bent pieces and enjoy the spicy fragrance of the green wood. Durability is poor to moderate, 2 to 4 years.

- *Location:* Old fields and in roadsides from New York and Vermont south to central Florida and west to Oklahoma and Texas. It is found in limited cultivation in other areas as a novelty tree.

- *Disadvantage:* Does not bend well.

Sumac, Fragrant

(Rhus aromatica)

This native shrub grows up to 10 feet high and as wide and is sometimes planted to attract wildlife. The small clusters of red berries do not look like the other sumac varieties' seed clusters (these are rounded and small, whereas most of the other sumacs have tall, pointed berry clusters), and the trifoliate leaves may look more like poison ivy upon a casual glance, although the plant grows differently.

The wood of this shrub is excellent for small trellises due to the very flexible nature of the limbs. You can easily make intricate bends and twists in project designs. Durability is moderate to good, 3 to 5 years.

- *Location:* Grows naturally in sandy and rocky soils from Quebec south to Florida and west to Kansas, Oklahoma, and surrounding states.

- *Disadvantage:* The wood, when freshly cut, has a strong odor. Once it dries, the fragrance disappears, but until then it may be objectionable — hence its other name, stinking sumac.

Sycamore

(Platanus occidentalis)

Also called American plane tree, the sycamore is sometimes used as a landscape tree in cities due to its tolerance of pollution. The tree is seldom used in home landscapes because its shedding of bark and twigs, and its very large leaves require a lot of maintenance. Sycamore trees can grow to an enormous size, have beautiful white bark on the upper branches, and are excellent shade trees.

Sycamore wood, when found growing in large colonies close together, can be useful in trellis making, as it is flexible and easily bent into gentle arches. Even though the wood is listed as tough and dense in tree guides, the young wood doesn't weather well outdoors and has little strength in the saplings. Durability is poor, 1 to 3 years.

- **Location:** Grows naturally along streams, in valleys and on hillsides, but it will grow in almost any kind of soil. It is found from southwest Maine, New York, southern Ontario, Michigan, Iowa, and eastern Nebraska south to Florida and Texas, as well as throughout the central Mississippi Valley. Durability is 1 to 3 years.

- **Disadvantages:** Very little strength when dry.

Willow

(Salix spp.)

Willow limbs are a delight to work with, and the corky-smooth texture makes this wood one of the most enjoyable to use for a variety of projects. Second-growth willow — young trees (up to 4–6 inches in diameter) that are cut to about knee-high and allowed to grow up with multiple sprouts — is excellent for bentwood projects. The practice of cutting willow and allowing it to grow back will create a harvestable wood that can be cut again and again for more projects, with no apparent harm to the tree. (Basket makers have used this practice for centuries.)

Willow is pliable, flexible, and easily bent into complex shapes. When using willow for furniture or trellises, woodworkers generally choose a stronger wood, such as hickory or oak, for the crosspieces and main structure, using the weaker, more pliable willow for the curves and intricate bends. Durability is moderate to excellent, 3 to 8 years.

Weeping willow *(Salix babylonica)* is outstanding for small trellises, as the long limbs work well for intricate bends. Weeping willow is one of the best natural materials for weaving baskets, and wonderful small trellis designs can be executed using this material. Durability outdoors is moderate, 3 to 5 years or longer, depending on size.

- **Location:** Various willow species can be found throughout the United States and into Canada and Mexico. Willow grows near streams, ponds, and other wet places in a wide variety of climates and conditions. Some varieties are used as landscape plants, while others are used to control stream erosion. This is an easy wood to cultivate from cuttings and grow for your own use (see Resources).

- **Disadvantage:** Not as strong as some other woods where an inflexible, straight piece is needed.

Common Vines

Though not the most desirable trellis-making materials, many vines will work for some projects, depending on the size and durability desired.

Bittersweet, Chinese

(Celastrus orbiculatus)

In some parts of the country, especially the New England states, where this non-native bittersweet was used as a landscape plant, it has become a tenacious and troublesome weed. If left unchecked, the vines will cover landscape or timber trees and shrubs with leaves that close out the sun, and the larger vines will eventually kill even large trees. The long, even-sized vines work well for basket weaving and small trellis making, and harvesting the vines actually saves the environment around them from sure death. Durability is 2 to 3 years or longer, depending on size of the material used.

- *Location:* This non-native bittersweet grows wherever it was planted in the landscape and has escaped cultivation, particularly along coastal areas.

- *Disadvantages:* Grows back rapidly and is difficult to eradicate. Not recommended for straight pieces on trellises, as it has very little strength.

Honeysuckle

(Lonicera spp.)

This vine has some of the same disadvantages as grapevine, but honeysuckle can be useful in combination with a basic trellis structure. Winding a vine such as honeysuckle around the structural

Why Grapevine Cannot Be Used

Maybe it's because grapevine (*Vitis* spp.) wreaths are popular, or because more people have access to grapevines, but people often say to me, "Grapevines make really good trellises, don't they?" The answer is "No!" It is true that grapevines are readily available across the country, but this is a very poor material for trellises.

Two factors make grapevine a really useless material for bentwood projects. The first is that grapevines grow in an upward spiral, winding themselves around things as they stretch toward the sun. Because of this spiraling habit, there are always bends in several directions (rather than the gentle curves of a weighted limb or the straightness of a sapling). These 360-degree bends, crooks, and curves make it very difficult to create a graceful trellis from this material.

The second factor is that grapevines do not last long outside once cut. A trellis may last a year or a little longer, but there is little strength to the wood once it has weathered.

pieces of a simple trellis can give it more bulk and interest. Durability is 2 to 3 years when used on a trellis structure.

- **Location:** Found on roadsides, where it has been used for erosion control and escaped into fields; along edges of fields; and in old orchards, as well as in lawns, where it has escaped or was formerly used for landscape purposes. Some varieties are native to the Midwest and South. Shrubby varieties have been planted for landscaping and are not generally useful for trellis work.

- **Disadvantages:** Too curvy and small for the actual trellis structure. Little strength when dry.

Rattan Vine

(Berchemia scandens)

This is also called strangler vine, due to the plant's habit of twining itself around small saplings, strangling them as it tightens around the trunk and covering the top. Rattan vine is a tough, curving, twisting vine that is not useful for the basic structure of a trellis but is outstanding to give the structure bulk and interest. The vines can be unwound from saplings and bushes, clipped off, and then wound around the trellis structure. The wood is substantial enough to nail or wire easily and can be manipulated to fit almost any shape. Durability is moderate, 3 to 5 years.

- **Location:** Rattan vine grows along lakes and streams in rocky and poor soil, as well as at the edges of abandoned fields, throughout the lower Mississippi Valley and surrounding areas.

- **Disadvantage:** If bent sharply and nailed, the wood may split after it dries, although that does not detract from the trellis.

Wisteria, American

(Wisteria frutescens)

Wisteria has fewer crooks and turns than grapevine, is often straighter-growing when it is climbing, and will last a bit longer outside after it is cut and made into a project. Durability is 2 to 3 years or longer.

- **Location:** Grown as a landscape plant throughout the United States and has escaped cultivation in some areas.

- **Disadvantages:** Not especially long-lasting (2–3 years), and little strength for straight, structural pieces.

Vines to Avoid

Grapevine wreath makers learn to identify poison ivy (*Rhus radicans*) and poison oak (*Rhus toxicodendron*) early on in their craft. Wreaths are often made in winter, when leaves are off the vines and trees. If you are going to make trellises in winter (which is an excellent time, because it is easier to see the structure of the saplings), you should learn how to identify poison ivy and poison oak, too. Many people are allergic to the oils, and simply brushing against the wood is enough to cause a severe skin reaction. Both of these plants grow in many regions throughout the United States. They are easily identified by their wood and the way they grow. Ask for help from your local forester or conservation agent, or consult a good guidebook if you are unsure about identification.

CHAPTER 2

Making the Basic Trellis

All my trellis designs are based on one basic shape — the simple rectangle. Once you have mastered the process of joining the angles of uprights and crosspieces with nails and wire (as described in this chapter), you can then turn that basic rectangle into beautiful and functional trellises, gates, fences, and arbors, as shown in the designs in chapters 3 through 7.

The Tools You Need

It's important to get your tools and materials ready before you begin to build your trellis. Although it isn't necessary to buy expensive tools for this project, it is important that you have adequate tools for the job, that they work with some ease and precision, and that they be comfortable. The difference between using a good tool that works well in your hands and using a bargain or hand-me-down tool is like the difference between cooking in a well-equipped kitchen and cooking on a rock beside a campfire on a riverbank. The right tools can make your project pleasant and enjoyable rather than frustrating and discouraging. Following are my recommendations.

Hammer

You need a light- to medium-weight carpenter's hammer — the type used for light carpentry work such as driving nails into wood. Old, worn hammers or ones intended for upholstery work, rock work, metalwork, or mechanical and automotive work will not do a good job. A hammer that is too light can slow you down, causing you to have to pound harder to drive the nails and thus resulting in more bent nails, more nails flying through the air, and more frustration. If you don't have a good, light- to medium-weight carpenter's hammer, buy one.

Pliers

A new pair of pliers is not quite as important as a new hammer, but you should have pliers that (1) easily grasp and hold wire without slipping off while you twist, and (2) cut wire easily with one cutting motion (rather than chewing and bending the wire). Old, worn-out pliers that are loose and slip apart or that no longer have a good grip in the mouth (where the two pieces grasp the wire) will slow you down. You can get an adequate pair of pliers for $5 to $8, and these will serve you well in your trellis making and installation.

Loppers or Pruning Saw

My personal preference is to use loppers for cutting down larger saplings and for cutting the uprights and crosspieces to size. Sawing takes longer and is more tiring on my arms. Others have told me they like to use a pruning saw because it is more comfortable for them. It's a matter of choice, but my recommendation is to get a good pair of loppers that are sharp and will open large enough to hold and cut something about the

size of the cardboard roll for paper towels (approximately 1½ to 1¾" in diameter).

Hand Pruners

There are lots of excellent hand pruners on the market, and yet I have often observed homeowners using old scissors for pruning. Antique pruners also seem to be attractive to some. I have used the pruners my father had for 50 years, and all they are good for is making me very angry because they are so dull and worn-out and they pinch the heel of my hand.

Some of the newer pruners on the market have nifty features such as soft, comfortable handles; handles that swivel to prevent blisters; and a gear-lever action that makes cutting very easy. If you are going to make more than one trellis and do not own a comfortable pair of pruners, I recommend purchasing a good, efficient pair.

Protective Gloves

A sturdy pair of cloth or leather gloves will make parts of this work more comfortable. I suggest wearing gloves to protect your hands when wiring and cutting the wood, then taking them off for holding the small nails during the nailing process.

The Materials You Need

The materials you need for making a trellis are minimal. I suggest you assemble all these ahead of time, so that once you're ready to work, you can move right along without having to run to the hardware store.

Wire

The easiest and least expensive wire to use is "tie wire" (also "ty wire"), available at lumberyards. It's used to tie reinforcing rods together in concrete work. Some of the self-serve home lumber stores may list this as 16-gauge black wire. Either way, it is a soft, workable wire, usually sold in two roll sizes and costing between $2 and $4. The wire will rust quickly, causing it to be almost invisible on your finished trellis.

Large Nails

For attaching medium-sized or larger pieces of wood together at joints, I use nails that are sold in hardware or lumber stores as "Sheetrock nails." They are very sharp, lightly galvanized, and about 1¼ to 1½ inches long. An added feature is that they are inexpensive. These nails work well on wood pieces about ¾ to 1 inch in diameter.

If you are using larger pieces of wood (more than 1 inch in diameter), you will need a few larger nails. Larger nails are identified by gauge and sold by the pound. I use 12- or 14-gauge nails for larger pieces of wood. It doesn't matter whether you use galvanized or nongalvanized

nails, as rusting makes little difference on the trellis and can even be an advantage — rusted nails are almost invisible.

Small Nails

The other kind of nail I always have on hand when building a trellis is termed a "brite nail." These nails are sold in hardware and discount stores by 2-ounce box (rather than by the pound, as with large nails). A good size for most decorative pieces, including the smaller bentwood pieces, lattice, and the like, is a ⅞-inch nail. A 2-ounce box sells for less than $1.50. Brite nails are sharp and easily driven. Bend them over on the back after driving them through the material. They will rust and become nearly invisible over time.

If you are making smaller trellises, such as those used for a desktop planter, you should have a package of ½-inch nails, as well. These are too short for the average garden trellis because the nail must go all the way through the first piece of wood and nearly all the way through the other piece (completely through the second piece is more preferable) for a strong joint. To be on the safe side, buy a small package of both ½-inch and ⅞-inch nails to have on hand.

Making a Work Space

The ideal work space is an old wooden picnic table outside in the yard. You can nail into a picnic table without causing much damage, and the boards give you guidelines for estimating the squareness and size of the trellis as you build.

My old picnic table doesn't look that great anymore, and I have meant to replace it with a better one for some time. But it is so perfect for trellis making that I just keep giving it another coat of paint every year and making more trellises, all of which gives it a pleasant antique quality that a new table just wouldn't have.

Another option for a trellis work space is any table that is a comfortable height for you, with a piece of plywood on top. The plywood doesn't need to be any larger than about 12 inches by 12 inches and ¾ to 1 inch thick. All you need is a place to nail the joints, and the plywood can be moved around easily. When I give workshops, I sometimes use a folding conference table, with just a small piece of plywood to protect the surface.

Working outdoors makes it especially easy to clean up afterward. If you are working in a garage, it is also easy to sweep up the trimmings and dust. Regardless of the space you choose, you will need enough room to move the long saplings and emerging trellis with ease without knocking things off the wall.

A Note on Materials

A Wood Materials List is provided for each project. Part Names, Number (of pieces), and Length should be closely studied before gathering wood. Because Diameter will vary according to the type of wood selected (see page 4 for Common Types of Wood), only general recommendations are given.

The Basic Trellis

This basic trellis has a finished height of 7 to 8 feet, large enough for clematis or scarlet runner beans. This sounds huge, but it will seem much smaller when it is in the garden. The assembly of this piece is the foundation for all the trellis designs in this book. Once you've mastered the basics, the decorative variations are endless.

Wood Materials List			
Part Name	Number	Length	Diameter
Side uprights*	2	12–14'	Approx. 1¾" at the larger (bottom) end, tapering to about the size of your little finger
Crosspieces	4	3'	Approx. 1¾"
Center upright	I	7–8'	Approx. 1½"
Decorative pieces	4 or 5 (more for an elaborate trellis)	6'	About the size of your thumb

*Flexible.

1. Planning Your Design

Before you get carried away with the process of making the trellis, first make a simple sketch of what you want your trellis to look like. This will help you visualize both how the trellis will look as it progresses and how it will be assembled.

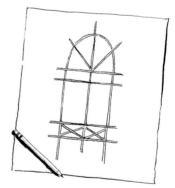

2. Gathering the Wood

Using your sketch, make a checklist of all the pieces of wood you will need to gather. Note which ones need to be flexible and which ones are straight crosspieces. (For an 8' finished height, side uprights should be 12–14' long to allow for sufficient bending.) Then gather the wood you need.

Before bringing home your wood, check to make sure the pieces intended to be flexible will indeed bend. Bend the uprights once or twice into the simple upper arch you will make (see step 8) to be sure they will bend that far. If a piece breaks, cut another kind of wood. It's better to find out early on that the wood isn't flexible enough than to discover that halfway through the project.

Cut a few extra pieces of wood to ensure that you have enough on hand. As the trellis shape emerges, you may be overcome with creativity and want to add more material. Embellishment, after all, is what these trellises are all about, so don't feel that you need to restrain yourself or your creativity.

Nailing Tip

Before placing your uprights on the work surface, put down a piece of scrap wood that is wide enough for the trellis wood to rest on. This will give you a secure nailing surface, and the nails will go in much easier.

3. Laying Out the Side Uprights

Using your rough design sketch as a reference, lay the two side uprights parallel to each other on a worktable (or firm, flat surface), about 24" apart and with the thicker ends even with the end of the table near where you are standing.

4. Attaching the Lower Crosspiece

Lay a crosspiece across the two uprights about 16" from the end of the table (and ends of the uprights). Center this piece so that about 12" extends beyond each side. Don't worry about cutting off the excess at this point. Nail the crosspiece in place with nails that are long enough to go all the way through the crosspiece and most or all the way through the upright.

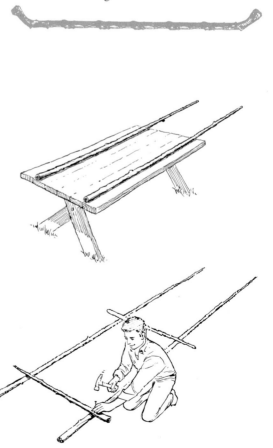

5. Attaching the Upper Crosspiece

Lay the second crosspiece across the uprights, about 40" to 45" from the lower crosspiece. Adjust all the pieces as needed to get the whole structure square, with the crosspieces at right angles to the uprights. When you have the second crosspiece positioned, nail it in place at both joints.

6. Securing the Joints

With pliers and tie wire, secure the four nailed joints. Cut off a piece of wire about 6" long and go around the joint, catching both pieces of wood. Twist the wire with the pliers until it is as tight as possible (the tighter the better). Cut off some of the excess wire and bend the rest out of the way.

Wiring is necessary to strengthen the joints, giving the trellis a bit more stability and ensuring that the nails will hold. The wood will shrink about 25 percent in 2 weeks, so you will probably need to retighten or rewire these joints at that point.

The Basic Rectangle

Once you have securely attached the two crosspieces to the two uprights, you have a relatively squared rectangle with the uprights sticking out the top. This structure is the basic foundation for just about any trellis, gate, or small fence you will build. Since this is the foundation, be sure to get it as square as possible. If the crosspieces do not look symmetrical with the uprights, it is easy at this point to pull out the nails, reposition the pieces, and nail again.

7. Bending Down the Nails

Turn the entire trellis rectangle over and hammer down any nail ends that may be sticking out the back. Return the trellis to the "front" side (which you were working on).

8. Bending the Uprights into an Arch

If any step of the trellis project is going to be difficult, this is the one. You have two choices: (1) ask for some help holding the pieces as you bend them; or (2) bend one piece of the small end of the upright over and temporarily tie it, then bend the other one over, and secure the two together.

Before beginning, it is a good idea to drive a nail through the two side uprights into the work surface. This gives you some leverage as you bend the uprights and keeps the trellis from flopping around on the table.

Readjust the arch if necessary and wire it securely into position. Wire the two bent pieces together about every 8" around the arch, twisting the wire tightly to secure it. Your basic structure is finished.

Shaping Your Arch

Bend both uprights and *lightly* tie the pieces in place. Now step back and look at the arch you have made. Is it too pointy at the top (a)? Does it look more like a squashed arch than a pretty trellis top (b)? Or are the proportions just right (c)?

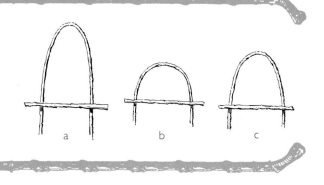

a   b   c

9. Attaching the Center Upright

With the trellis lying flat on the table, crosspieces down, position the center upright in the middle, with about 6" of the thicker end extending below the bottom crosspiece. (Don't worry about how much of the top end extends beyond the arch. You will cut off the excess.) Nail the upright into position at each crosspiece, but don't nail into the arch (nailing may split the bent wood). Instead, wire the joint where the upright crosses the arch.

10. Attaching Additional Crosspieces

Turn the trellis over and position an additional crosspiece 6" above the lower one. Nail it to the uprights and wire the joints securely.

Position the last crosspiece 6" below the upper crosspiece, then nail and wire it in place. Turn the trellis over and bend over any nail points sticking out the back. Leave the trellis facedown.

11. Attaching the Lattice Pieces

Beginning with the thinner end of one of your decorative pieces, cut a piece long enough to fit diagonally across one of the rectangles formed by the two bottom crosspieces and the middle upright. Nail it in place, then trim off any excess with hand pruners.

Cut another piece of equal length from the same branch, place it diagonally across the rectangle to form an X, and nail it in place. Repeat the process to form an X in the other rectangle on the other side of the center upright.

Tips for Working with Wire

* When you are finished wiring each joint, cut off the excess wire and bend the rest out of the way.

* Hide the wire behind the trellis. (You will notice that the trellis has a front and a back as you work.) Wire can also be hidden from view by positioning it underneath the limbs at what will become the lower portion of the trellis, which won't be seen when the trellis is installed in the garden.

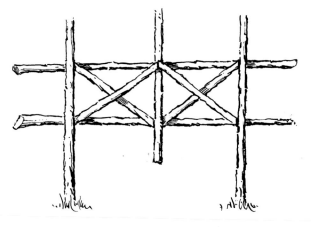

12. Attaching the Fan Pieces

Turn the trellis over, with the crosspieces facing up. Cut two decorative pieces about 3' long. Position the bottom of one end at the intersection of the top crosspiece and the center upright, with the limb extending up at about a 45-degree angle across one side of the arch. Hide the bottom end behind the center upright and nail it in place. Place the other limb in the same position on the other side of the arch. Nail it in place. Securely wire the upper ends of the limbs to the arch. (Do not nail into the arch, as nailing may split the arch.)

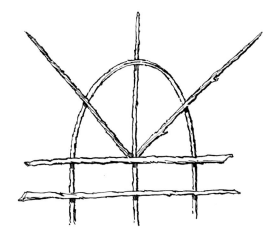

13. Trimming and Finishing

Trim off the ends of all the crosspieces to leave about 12" extending over each side upright. Trim the fan pieces and center upright to leave about 18" (or whatever is visually pleasing to you) extending beyond the arch.

If you want to embellish the design, you can add more latticework or other decorative pieces. Or you can incorporate some of the elements from one of the designs in chapter 3.

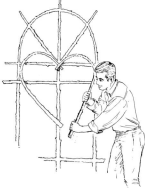

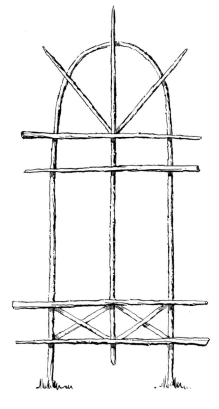

Securing Your Trellis in the Ground

There are several options for installing your trellis in the garden. You can use metal posts, wooden stakes, metal rods (such as pieces of reinforcing rod), or plastic rods. Make sure that whatever you choose is sunk 16 to 18 inches into the ground (for an 8-foot trellis) so that the trellis is secure.

Metal Posts

Metal garden posts (also known as V and T posts because of their shape when viewing them from the end) are most resistant to being blown over. They come in sizes ranging from 36 inches to 7 feet. For a 7- to 8-foot-high trellis, use a 36- or 48-inch post driven into the ground so that the metal plate is just below ground level.

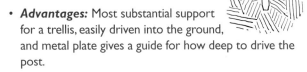

- *Advantages:* Most substantial support for a trellis, easily driven into the ground, and metal plate gives a guide for how deep to drive the post.

- *Disadvantage:* Cost is about $2 per post and metal posts may require repainting to match the trellis.

Wooden Stakes

You can make your own wooden stakes by cutting two 4-foot-long pieces of wood that are slightly larger in diameter than a broom handle. Drive each stake 16 to 18 inches into the ground with a large hammer. Place them the same distance apart as the trellis's main side uprights.

- *Advantage:* Little or no cost except the time for cutting.

- *Disadvantage:* Could split as you drive them into the ground, or may break off at ground level.

Metal Rods

Metal rods are available in ½-inch and ⅝-inch diameter. (There are other sizes, too, but these sizes are the best for this purpose.). I have found 3- and 4-foot lengths at some home supply stores. At lumberyards and contractor's supply stores, reinforcing rods generally come in standard 21-foot lengths, but most suppliers will cut pieces to size for a small fee.

- *Advantage:* Easy to drive into the ground; rust-brown color blends with trellis color.

- *Disadvantage:* None. Just be sure to wear gloves, since the ends may be sharp where the rods were cut.

Plastic Rods

Green plastic rods are available at discount stores and garden centers. They look just like reinforcing rods and come in lengths from 24 inches to 6 feet. They can be used for smaller trellises, but because of their flexibility, they do not work well for a larger trellis unless it is positioned near a building for additional support.

- *Advantage:* Readily available.

- *Disadvantages:* Flexible and a bit hard to drive; colors vary.

Installing Your Trellis

Select the spot for your trellis, taking into consideration what you plan to grow on it and its visibility. (After all, you want it to be seen and enjoyed.)

1. Driving in the Post

With a heavy hammer, drive one post or stake 16" to 18" into the ground at the approximate point where one of the the trellis uprights will be. Hold one trellis upright against the post you have just driven and mark the spot where the other trellis upright touches the ground (or use a tape measure). Set the trellis aside.

2. Where you marked the spot, drive the second post into the ground to approximately the same depth as the first post.

3. Wiring the Trellis to the Post

Position the trellis against the two posts, with the trellis uprights in front of the posts. Find a spot 3" to 4" from the top of the post and wire the upright to the post at this point. Then firmly wire the bottom of that upright to the post about 12" from the ground. You should now have one trellis upright wired securely to one post.

4. Repeat the same process with the other post and upright, securely wiring the trellis in place. Your trellis is now installed, and you are ready to start growing plants on it (see chapter 8).

CHAPTER 3

Decorative Trellis Designs

This chapter includes twenty-two trellis designs based on the basic trellis in chapter 2. Some are simple and require only minimal green, flexible wood; others require more workable wood and more bending on your part. Start with one of the simpler designs before trying the more intricate ones. Sometimes the wood you are using has a mind of its own. In that case, adapt your design to fit the materials. More important, have fun with the project. If it gets frustrating, sit down, have a glass of iced tea, and catch your breath. It will make the project go much easier.

Adapting the Size

Many of the designs in this chapter are adaptable. They can be created as full-sized 7- to 8-foot trellises or can be scaled down for a 4- to 5-foot trellis. Some can even be made into miniature trellises for the planter or desktop. But beware: Miniature trellises are often more difficult to make and harder for the beginner than full-sized ones.

Loop-de-loop

This is a fairly simple trellis that doesn't require a lot of pieces. It's best to use two long uprights for the main arch, rather than trying to make it from one piece. The loop-de-loop pieces and bottom braces are attached to the back of the trellis after the crosspieces are added.

Size: 8' high and 40" wide

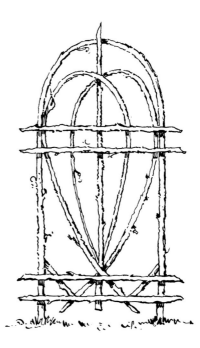

Heart and Diamonds

This a very sturdy trellis, since the primary design elements are a series of braces running from the center upright to the side uprights and crosspieces. None of the brace pieces has to be flexible. All of the pieces making up the descending diamonds and triangles are attached to the back of the trellis. The arched heart and the decorative pieces along the lower crosspieces are applied to the front.

Size: Approx. 8' high and 40" wide; this can be scaled down to make a 4'-high trellis or even a miniature trellis for a planter.

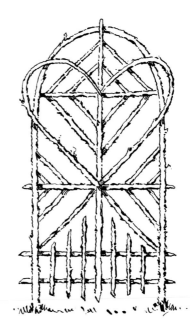

Butterfly

This simple design has graceful curves and elegant lattice-work. The various-sized upper and lower lattice pieces are all applied to the back of the trellis where the cut ends are hidden behind the crosspieces. The two Xs in the center of the trellis are applied from the front, ends tucked behind the crosspieces and side uprights. The arched "butterfly wings" are made from four flexible pieces, wired to the front of the main arch, with the bottom ends tucked behind the intersection of the center upright and upper crosspiece. Morning glories really show off the design.

Size: 7' to 8' high and 35" to 40" wide

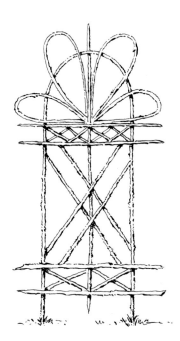

Bighearted

Here's a good chance to practice making a heart shape. Once you have your basic rectangle with the crosspieces, attach the fan pieces to the top and the smaller decorative pieces on the lower crosspieces. Then secure the two cross-piece braces to the back of the trellis. Finish by attaching the bentwood heart to the front, just below the upper crosspiece. Cardinal climber or mandevilla gives this trellis a look of antiquity.

A nice variation on the bighearted trellis introduces lat-ticework applied to the back of the lower crosspieces (see inset). It looks best with moonvine or morning glories.

Size: 8' high and 35" to 40" wide

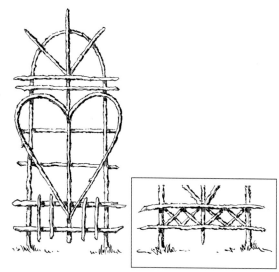

Forming an Arched Heart

To create hearts or other decorative bends for your trellis, use branches that are very flexible and taper from the size of your index finger down to the size of a pencil. (See the section on wood selection in chapter 1, including vines used for trellis work.) Experiment with two similar-sized pieces to make sure they will bend well. Nail or wire the end of one piece in place, then bend it into one half of the shape you want, wiring it in place as you go. Repeat with the other piece to form the other half of the design. Once you get a feel for bending wood, you will be more comfortable creating more elaborate designs.

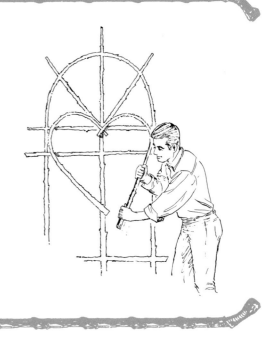

Two of Hearts

Native cedar or hickory works well for this full-sized trellis. Both woods, when green and freshly cut, are easily bent. Attach the angled braces for stability before applying the large heart to the front, beginning at the back of the lower crosspiece. Finish by attaching the smaller heart near the bottom.

Size: 7' to 8' high and 32" to 38" wide

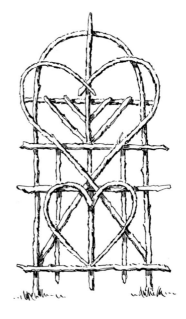

Hobbit Home

This simple design is made up of three arches. It is best to use two uprights, joined together, for each arch to give the arch uniformity and consistent strength on both sides of the trellis. For an 8' trellis, use two uprights 12' to 14' long for the large arch, two pieces 10' to 12' long for the medium arch, and two pieces 8' long for the small inner arch. The diamond pattern in the center is applied to the back of the center arch.

Size: 7' to 8' high and 35" to 40" wide

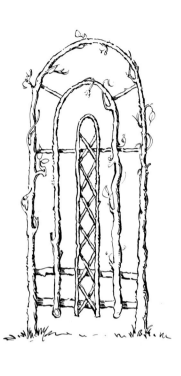

Dream Catcher

Adapted from a Native American design, this trellis is wonderful to look at in the early morning when helpful garden spiders have spun webs to catch bugs during the night. Take a cup of tea outside and enjoy the diamond-like dewdrops as they glisten on the webs in the morning sun.

Begin by joining the side uprights with the crosspieces, then attach the center upright on the back. The upper reverse arch is made from one piece, as is the lower arch. The only somewhat difficult part is making the center circle. Think of it as a wreath in wood and use two or more pieces to form a circle that is as perfectly round as possible. Once the circle is in place, apply the two crosspieces to the back of it to form an X. Bend smaller branches inside each "pie" section to form the six inner arches representing the web; wire in place.

Size: 7' high at the corner uprights and 32" to 38" wide

Happy Heart

The latticework and small pieces applied to the back of this trellis also act as braces. Put them in place, then trim off the ends evenly with hand pruners. The inner double arch near the top is formed by joining two pieces to the upper arch and center upright.

Size: 7' to 8' high and 30" wide

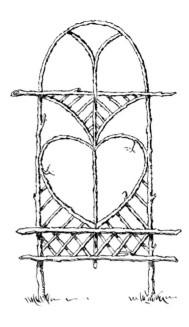

Stack of Hearts

This design is reminiscent of the late Victorian era, with lots of graceful bent wood. Hickory or native cedar, even elm or alder, work well for this trellis. For the hearts, the first choice would be willow, red-twig dogwood, or fragrant sumac (see chapter 1).

Once you have the crosspieces in place, apply the decorative arches to the back of the bottom crosspieces, then work up from the bottom of the trellis. Apply the bottom heart first, using two flexible pieces, and finish with the smaller, top hearts, made the same way and wired in place.

Size: 7' tall and 30" wide

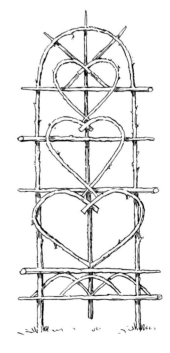

Fifties-Style Garden

This simple trellis requires minimal bending. Any green wood that bends slightly could be used for the upper and lower bent pieces. Either green or dry wood can be used for the rest of the pieces. Join the two side uprights with the crosspieces first, then add the center upright to the front. Attach the bottom arched piece to the sides and center upright. Then attach the two additional uprights to the back of the trellis before making the arched pieces on the top.

Use this trellis by itself or make several and attach them side by side to form a fence or larger background trellis, creating a 1950s look in the garden.

Size: 6' high and 4' wide

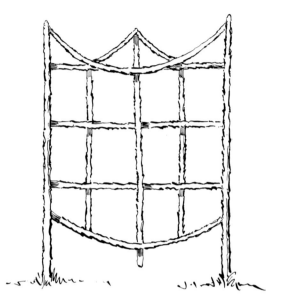

China Moon

Chinese designs, adapted by the English and Americans, were very popular in the United States in the late 1800s. This simple trellis has a slightly Eastern look. Make a circle from two or three pieces of willow for the "moon" at the top. The remainder of the trellis is made up of simple additions to the basic shape, using whatever materials you have available.

Size: 7' to 8' high and 35' to 40' wide

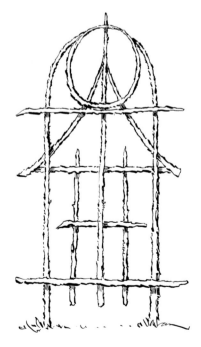

Lattice-Be-Loved

Hearts were very popular in gardens of the past. People believed that a trellis should do more than simply hold up a vine; it should inspire, raise the spirits, and add cheer. The intricate latticework on this trellis does just that. Not complicated to do, it's just a bit more time-consuming than some others because of the added lattice. The result is a strong structure that can support honeysuckle or hyacinth vines. Consider daintier vines like canary vine, cardinal climber, or climbing snapdragon.

Size: 7' to 8' high and 30" to 36" wide; it can be made smaller for other locations.

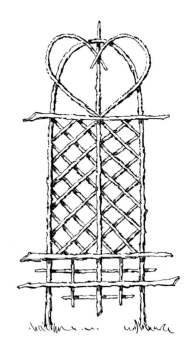

Traditional Fan

There is not much bent about the wood in this trellis, save for the somewhat bent crosspieces. It can be made from almost any kind of green wood (or a combination of green and dry), even ash, which will bend slightly but will break if bent at sharper angles. Attach two side uprights to the center upright by nailing and wiring them in place at the bottom, approximately 12" above the end of the center upright. You should now have one center upright and two side pieces in a V or fan shape. Attach the arches, bending them slightly, starting at the top and working downward to the base. Wire the arches securely in place, nailing them at the center and ends. Then secure the two remaining uprights, one on each side of the center upright.

Be sure to use something substantial to install this trellis because it has only one true upright. A 6' metal post driven

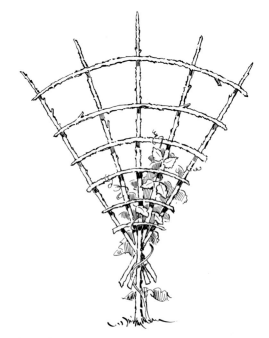

into the ground will work well (see page 26).

Size: 4' high and 26" wide, 6' high and 30" wide, or 8' high and 40" wide, depending on your needs

Eternity's Door

This basic rectangle can be built out of any kind of wood, even dry wood, except for the arch, which should be made from two pieces of green, flexible wood. Begin by building the rectangular frame, add the center upright, and then apply the angled pieces, hiding the cut ends behind the side and center upright. Finally, apply the simple arch in front, over the angled pieces. Nail *and* wire several of the joints for extra strength. The bigger this trellis is, the more effective it will be at the back of a flower bed or next to a wall.

Size: 7' to 8' high and 40" wide

Gothic Arches

This is another simple trellis. You will need two flexible uprights, 12' to 14' long, for the two main uprights. The center arch, attached to the back of the crosspieces, requires two flexible uprights 8' to 10' long. The three crosspieces and the two half-arches, applied over the front of the cross-pieces, can be made of any available material, even wood that bends only slightly. The delicate lines look good with small-leaved vines, but the trellis is sturdy enough to support heavier vines such as hyacinth and some kinds of ivy.

Size: 7' to 8' high and 38" to 45" wide

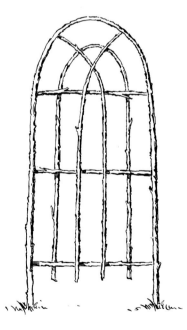

Victorian Lace

Use willow (or several pieces of other flexible wood) bent and wired in place to make these loops and hearts. This trellis is a bit more challenging than the others because of the way the loops twist. Two slender, very flexible saplings are used to make each large loop. For the other loops, attach several flexible pieces together by wiring them in position, overlapping the ends if necessary.

    Size: 7' to 8' high and 38" to 40" wide; a larger trellis can be made by connecting three arches together before adding the loops and hearts.

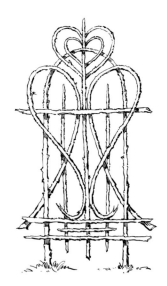

Roaring Twenties

This design makes an impressive background trellis or looks good attached to a wall. You could even use it indoors as a rustic decorating touch.

    Use the basic trellis structure (see chapter 2) to make three trellises, one that is 7' high and two that are 5' to 5½' high. The crosspieces and lattice pieces can be made from green or dry wood. The larger arch requires two short pieces that can be bent to form the half-arches between the center upright and the sides. Attach the three trellises together with wire.

    Size: 7' high and 5' wide

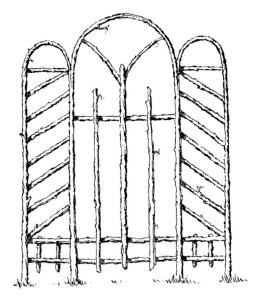

Three of Hearts

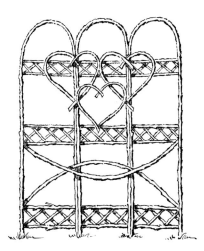

Three arches of the same size (approximately 7' high and 20–24" wide) are attached together to make this charming trellis. The lattice is applied from the back, while the hearts and two bent curves, or arches, at the bottom are applied on the front, after the rest of the trellis is completed.

    Size: 7' high and 5' wide

Elegantly Bent

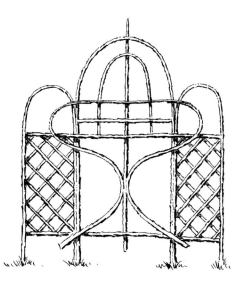

Two arched trellises (each 5' high and 20" wide) attached to a center trellis (7' high and 32" wide) make this design look difficult, but it is actually moderately simple. For the S curves, use green, very flexible wood that is small in diameter on the upper end. I used two pieces of slender native cedar, tied together in the middle, to make the upper crosspiece.

    Size: 7' high and 72" wide

Arch and Lattice

The three trellises that make up this design are exactly alike except that the middle one is 24" taller than the other two. The taller center piece has an X, or lattice, near the top but no lattice below, as the two smaller trellises placed in front furnish the lattice design. Very little truly flexible wood is required for this design, except for forming the arches themselves.

Size: 7' high and 56" to 60" wide

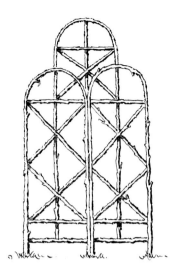

Graceful Loops

Practice making simpler trellises before you attempt this one. It requires some very flexible wood, such as willow or fragrant sumac, and a bit of patience. Make the loops carefully, wiring them in place as you bend. This classic Victorian trellis creates a sculptural background for your vines and flowers. Note that the two side arches overlap the middle arch a bit (about 6"). Assemble the three arches and attach them together with crosspieces before applying the loops. The crosspieces are behind the two smaller arches and in front of the large center arch.

Size: 7' high and approx. 56" wide

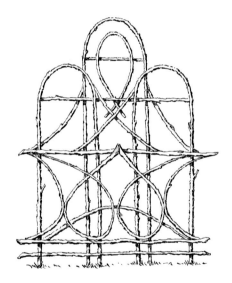

Entry Trellis
(Left Half)

This is one half of an entry trellis for a porch or entryway to a garden. I attached this to a porch post and made one facing the other way for the right side of the entry to Dairy Hollow House Restaurant in Eureka Springs, Arkansas. You could also use two crosspieces overhead, attaching them together to make an entryway and letting vines grow along the top. For this trellis, the lower arch (i.e., three lower crosspieces) spans to the center upright.

Size: Approx. 7' to 8' high and 5' wide

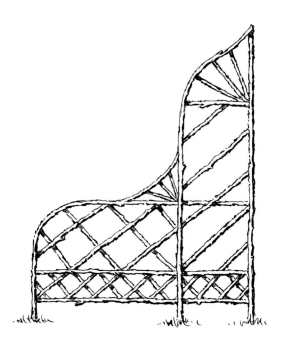

CHAPTER 4

Bentwood Gates

The gate is the guardian of the garden, a sentry to all who would enter. The gate says, "Stop here. Entry is limited." We had a gate when I was a child that divided the lawn area from where my pony was kept. The big gatepost was wide enough for my old cat, Tom, to sit on and watch sparrows as they scolded him away from their nests.

The gate itself was just a box frame with fence wire over it and a brace going diagonally from one corner to the other. Although I wasn't allowed in the area with the horse unless my parents were there, I could stand on the bottom rung of that gate and swing back and forth.

"Stop swinging on that gate!" my father shouted more than once, but it was much too tempting to stay

away. I knew better than to go beyond the gate, but I could pivot the old thing back and forth, knowing that just inches away was the forbidden area where I wanted to play.

Design a Gate to Fit the Purpose and Place

Gates serve all kinds of purposes, from keeping out animals to inviting people inside. A gate can convey a message. It can look welcoming, framing the plants inside and enticing the visitor to come into the garden. Or it can be a barrier, a stern reminder that before entering you must pass the guardian. Or a gate can be a shield, a curtain, as it were, to the drama on the other side. Gain passage through the gate, and the secrets are revealed.

But bentwood gates also can stand alone as a decorative addition to your garden, and they don't have to open and close if they're merely decorative. Decide on your needs and desires for a gate, then plan one that meets those requirements.

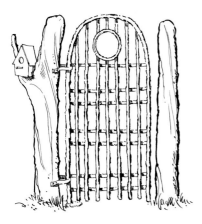

Bentwood gates can take many forms. They can be decorative and charming as well as functional. Depending on the kind of garden you have, you may choose a tall, substantial gate or a short, decorative one as part of a knee-high fence.

Bentwood gates look very attractive when placed under an archway, which directs the eye to the gate and guides entry into the garden.

Note on Measurements and Assembly

The lengths given for materials in these projects are slightly larger than the size of the finished gate. The excess is trimmed off when the gate is completed. I have not given exact measurements for the locations of the various pieces on each gate because wood can vary. Moreover, each builder should use his or her own sense of proportion as a guide. Use the illustrations to identify the approximate locations of the crosspieces, then make any visual adjustments that seem right to you.

Nail all the joints, then wire the major ones. More important than exactly where you place the limb or joint is that you have fun building your gate. You are the creator of the piece, so have confidence that your rustic bentwood gate will be a delight in your garden.

The Basic Gate

The bentwood gate is basically a trellis that swings, with slight variations. Most gates are about 3½ to 4 feet high when attached to a post. You need flexible wood for the arched pieces, just as you do for making a trellis. However, gates require more straight pieces for support and bracing. These pieces can be made from less flexible or even dry wood. Basically, you need two flexible uprights and at least three crosspieces for any gate. Each of the designs that appears in this chapter is accompanied by a complete wood materials list.

1. Creating a Design

Decide on a design (see pages 50–55) or create one of your own. Do a rough sketch on a piece of paper to get a feel for the lines. Decide how tall you want your gate to be. Remember, you can scale up or down any of the designs given here.

2. Gathering Your Materials

From your sketch, make a wood materials list. Include all the pieces you need, noting whether or not each piece needs to be bendable. Refer to chapter 2 for help in selecting and gathering your wood.

3. Laying Out the Uprights

If you are planning to put the gate in an established opening between two posts in a fence or row of plantings, measure the distance between the posts, then subtract about 8" (to allow space for the gate to hang and to attach the hinges). This will be the width of your gate. Lay your uprights on the work surface parallel to each other and this distance apart. Make sure the two thickest bottom ends are even with the edge of the table where you are standing.

If you do not have pre-existing posts, make the gate first to the desired size, then set the posts later to fit.

4. Attaching Two Crosspieces

Place a lower crosspiece, on top of the upright, about 8" from the bottom of the uprights, and nail it in place.

Position an upper crosspiece on top of the uprights, just below where you think the wood will start to bend when making the arch. This piece gives you leverage to bend the wood into the arch and provides much of the upper strength of the gate. Nail this piece securely to the uprights.

5. Securing the Joints

Wire the four joints you now have by wrapping a 6" piece of wire around both pieces of wood at each joint. Twist the ends together and tighten with pliers until the wire holds the joint firmly (the tighter the better). Cut off any excess wire and bend it out of the way.

6. Bending the Arch

If it is possible to nail through your gate frame to your worktable, I recommend doing so to stabilize the frame for this step. (Nail anywhere along the upright.) To form the arch, first bend the upper end of one upright over and wire it temporarily in place. Then bend the other upright over, matching the curve of the first one, to make a pleasing, complete arch. There is no hard-and-fast rule for how far you should bend the arch over. Use your eyes as your guide. Once you're happy with it, wire the two uprights together firmly at several places along the arch.

7. Attaching the Second Lower Crosspiece

For added bracing, place a second crosspiece about 8" above the lower one you have already attached. Securely nail and wire the crosspiece to the uprights. If desired, or if your design requires, add a second crosspiece about 6" below the existing upper crosspiece as well.

8. Attaching Additional Uprights

If your design has a center upright or a series of uprights, add them now. Nail them in place; it isn't necessary to wire them.

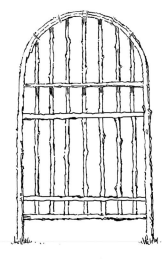

9. Adding Decorative Pieces

Now that you have your full frame in place, attach decorative pieces such as hearts, sunbursts, or other bentwood designs to the front. Nail them in place with small nails, then wire as needed.

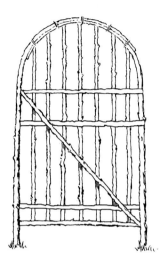

10. Attaching Bracing

Check to see that your gate is strong and sturdy. If it's not, add some additional bracing, such as a piece running from corner to corner, or angled pieces that will help keep the gate rigid when it is installed.

Bending Nails

Be sure to turn your trellis over periodically as you work, and hammer down any sharp nail points that may be sticking out the back.

Installing Your Gate

For most average-sized gates, you need two sturdy wooden posts, each about 7 to 8 feet long. (A very large gate will require longer posts.) The installed posts don't need to be any taller than 5 feet from the ground, and they can be shorter if necessary so that they are more visually appealing. You can use two posts cut from your own trees (with their own unique character), or you can buy precut posts. Standard fence posts available at lumberyards are 8 feet long. You will attach the gate to one post and, if desired, a latch to the other.

1. Digging the Post Holes

Determine the location for your gate and place a stake in the ground for the first post. Measure the total width of your gate and add approximately 8". Use this distance to determine the placement of your other post, then use a stake to mark the spot. Dig two holes, each about 20" to 24" deep, to sink the posts. Surround each post with rocks and tamp firmly in place or use concrete if you wish to make them permanent. When you have your posts in place, cut off the excess height. If you are using old, gnarled posts or plan to put a birdhouse on top of one post, 5' is a good height.

2. Installing a Base for Hinging the Gate

Place a flat rock, small concrete paver block (8 × 16 × 1"), or other hard surface that is at least 8 × 8 × 1" at the base of the post where you will hinge your gate.

The base can be left on top of the ground or sunken to be level with the soil's surface. It will serve as support for the gate, keeping it from sinking into the soil as it swings back and forth.

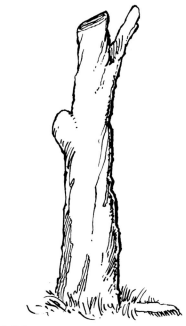

A flat rock or block, strategically placed, supports the gate.

3. Hanging the Gate

Cut two pieces of metal pipe hanger about 28" long. Prop your gate up on the base, and mark the spot on the front of the post that corresponds to the underside of the upper crosspiece. Nail one end of one piece of pipe hanger to this spot on the post.

Loop the other end of the pipe hanger around the gate upright just under the crosspiece, then nail the other end of the pipe hanger to the other side of the post. The pipe hanger isn't nailed to the gate itself, but it will act as a hinge for the gate.

Nail one end of the second piece of pipe hanger to the spot on the front of the post corresponding to the underside of the lower crosspiece (the top one if you have two lower pieces). Loop the pipe hanger just under the crosspiece and nail the other end to the back side of the post.

4. Attaching the Latch

If desired, attach a latch to the opposite post. Since the gate will not likely open and close in the wind, a latch may not be necessary.

Maintaining Your Gate

After a few weeks have passed and the wood has shrunk, check the joints on your gate and tighten the wires at each one. After the gate has aged for a few months, you may want to apply a clear wood preservative, such as that used on decks and other wood that is left outdoors. Brush on one or more coats and repeat annually if desired. Your gate can last for many years.

Happy Home

A gnarled gatepost, topped with a birdhouse, adds to the charm of this gate. Morning glories growing around the post add even more cheer to your garden entry.

Attach the crosspieces to the side uprights and form the arch. Then attach the center upright and short angled pieces to the back. Finish by attaching the heart to the front with wire.

Size: 4' high and 32" wide

Wood Materials List			
Part Name	Number	Length	Diameter
Side uprights**	2	7'	*
Crosspieces	4	34"	*
Center upright	1	4'	*
Short angled pieces	7	Approx. 3–4'	*
Heart**	2	30"	*

*Varies with wood chosen; see chapter 1 for suggestions.
**Very flexible.

Hearts Reflected

This is a simple gate to build, requiring two side uprights to make the arch. The only other pieces needed for the gate structure are three crosspieces and four center uprights that are attached in front of the crosspieces. The two hearts are made of very flexible wood (such as willow, hickory, or cedar) about the thickness of your little finger. Note that it takes two pieces to make each heart. The hearts are wired at their joints and to the uprights they cross, rather than being nailed.

Size: 5' high and 32" wide

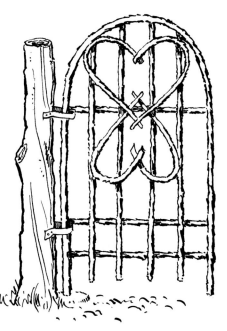

Wood Materials List			
Part Name	Number	Length	Diameter
Side uprights**	2	7–8'	*
Crosspieces	3	34"	*
Center uprights	4	5'	*
Hearts**	4	30–36"	*

*Varies with wood chosen; see chapter 1 for suggestions.
**Very flexible.

Good Morning, Sun

The sunburst design contributes to the strength of this gate. The two side uprights are first joined with the three crosspieces to form a sturdy frame for the gate, then bent to make the arch. Add the fourth crosspiece after forming the arched top. Attach the center upright and the two sunbeam pieces that form the basic X shape on the top. The X goes in front of the center upright. Next attach the sun oval, and attach the smaller sunbeam pieces behind and radiating out from the oval. The small arch is attached to the lower crosspieces and center upright. Then the short uprights are added. You can add a smaller design inside the lower arch if desired.

Size: 48" to 50" high and 32" wide

Wood Materials List			
Part Name	Number	Length	Diameter
Side uprights**	2	7–8'	*
Crosspieces	4	34"	*
Center upright	1	52" long	*
Sunbeam pieces	8	Approx. 30"	*
Sun circle**	1	Approx. 36–40"	*
Small arch uprights**	2	36"	About the size of your little finger
Short uprights	4	36–40"	*

*Varies with wood chosen; see chapter 1 for suggestions.
**Very flexible.

Along the Garden Path

This gate seems to say, "Come on in; walk along the garden path." It is quite simple to make. Begin by attaching the two side uprights to the top and bottom crosspieces. Bend the side uprights and make an arch. Next, add remaining three crosspieces, then attach the center upright to the back of the crosspieces. Attach the two inner arch uprights to the crosspieces, bend to form an arch, and wire in place. Finish by attaching the four fan pieces to the back of the upper arch. Scarlet runner beans climbing up the hinge side of the gate soften the edges.

Size: 50" high and 32" wide

Part Name	Number	Length	Diameter
Side uprights**	2	7–8'	*
Crosspieces	5	34"	*
Center upright	1	50" long	*
Inner arch uprights**	2	5–6'	*
Fan pieces	4	24"	*

Wood Materials List

*Varies with wood chosen; see chapter 1 for suggestions.
**Very flexible.

Triple Arch

This gate has a very simple but strong construction, reinforced by the large X in the middle and smaller Xs below. It is not really a functional gate (the open pattern won't keep out small dogs or other pets), but the design is classic and looks nice in almost any garden setting.

This project requires a minimal amount of wood. Begin by joining the side uprights and crosspieces, then forming the upper arch. Attach the center upright to the back of the frame, then attach the X cross brace. Add the lattice pieces, attaching them to the back of the two bottom cross-pieces. Finish by forming the small inner arches, wiring them in place.

Size: 50" high and 32" wide

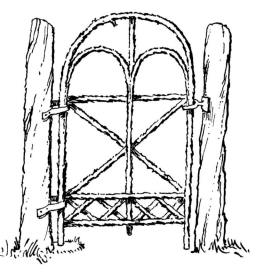

Wood Materials List			
Part Name	Number	Length	Diameter
Side uprights**	2	7–8'	*
Inner arch uprights**	2	7'	*
Center upright	1	50"	*
Crosspieces	3	36"	*
Cross braces	2	45"	*
Lattice pieces	8	Approx. 12"	*

*Varies with wood chosen; see chapter 1 for suggestions.
**Very flexible and strong.

Welcome to My Garden

This is a variation on the triple-arch gate, but with a slightly more efficient design for keeping pets out of the garden. The cross braces make this very sturdy, and the added uprights provide a barrier to keep out small animals. (*Note:* The part lengths given below are slightly longer than needed. You can trim off the excess when the gate is completed.)

Size: 45" to 50" high and 33" wide

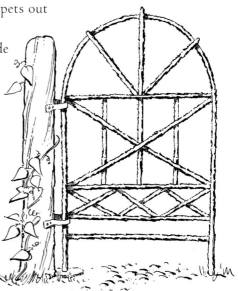

Wood Materials List			
Part Name	Number	Length	Diameter
Side uprights**	2	7½'	*
Crosspieces	4	34"	*
Cross braces	2	36"	*
Long upright	1	45"	*
Short uprights	2	22"	*
Fan pieces	2	24"	*
Lattice pieces	6	15–18"	*

*Varies with wood chosen; see chapter 1 for suggestions.
**Very flexible and strong.

CHAPTER 5

Bentwood Fences

A fence marks a line that divides one part of the yard from another. The fence can be purely decorative, adding artistic design to the foreground, or it can serve as a background for showing off specimen plants. A fence can be used to keep the dog out of the garden or the neighborhood kids from making a path across the lawn. A tall bentwood fence can add a feeling of privacy while not blocking the view. Or it can create a mini-climate for specific plants by dividing areas into sun and shade zones.

On the lawn of my childhood home, we had a large trellis fence we called the "great fence." It stood about 5½ feet high and 12 feet long. It was just a rectangle of lattice, simply crossed wood on a frame, but the two sides of the fence were vastly different.

On the east side, facing the morning sun, there was an oval goldfish pond at the base of the fence. It was deep enough that the water came up past my knees when I waded there, and it held water plants, frogs, and several sparkling orange goldfish that always nibbled at my ankles whenever I invaded their world.

On this side of the fence, my mother grew plants that liked afternoon shade. She had several roses, their colors protected by the light-filtering fence, and lady's-mantle, with its saucer-shaped leaves that held silvery drops of dew each morning. (I was told that fairies would drink the magical drops when no one was looking, and I spent hours trying to catch a peek of the wee people.) Nasturtiums and gladiolus, lobelias and sweet

Williams, all added color around the miniature pond.

Just inches away, on the west side of the lattice fence, grew tougher, heat-tolerant plants. There were zinnias and larkspurs; gomphrenas, daylilies and black-eyed Susans; ageratums, salvias, and large, bright yellow African marigolds, all thriving in the heat of the afternoon sun.

I was fascinated by how little climates were created just by the placement of the great fence. Morning glories grew across the top, their blue flowers opening to face the rising sun. Shrub roses and larger flowering shrubs grew happily at each end, and a vine-covered arch connected the trellis beds to the side of the house. It was one of my favorite places to play.

Variation on a Trellis

Like the gate designs in chapter 4, the fence designs in this chapter are variations of the basic trellis and are made in much the same way. A fence section, or panel, is constructed from crosspieces and uprights. This basic rectangle is then applied to several posts or supports, creating a fence.

Usually the rectangle of the fence panel is wider than it is tall. You might choose to make a fence 3 or 4 feet high, which would require sections about 6 or 7 feet long. Unless you have lots of wood on hand, you might want your fence to be about knee-high and purely decorative, since the larger the fence, the more material you will have to obtain.

Begin by reading the instructions for the decorative fence panel. Once you understand this construction, you are ready to try any of the variations that follow.

Decorative Fence Panel

This design is for one 4-foot panel of a simple decorative fence that is 24 inches high. Make as many of these panels as you need to complete the desired length of fence. The panels are joined together at the fence posts. Since most of the pieces in this design are straight wood, you can rely on dry wood or green wood that does not bend well for the major portion of the fence.

Size: Approx. 24" high and 4' wide; size varies according to materials used and needs of location.

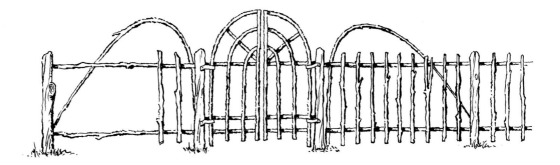

Wood Materials List			
Part Name	Number	Length	Diameter
Crosspieces	2	4½'	Approx. 1¾" at the large end
Uprights	Approx. 8–9	24"	*

*Varies with wood chosen; see chapter 1 for suggestions.

1. Laying Out the Crosspieces

Lay the two long crosspieces on your worktable. Place them parallel to each other, 18" apart, with the ends pointing in opposite directions (that is, the smaller end of one next to the larger end of the other). Adjust them so that the ends are even with each other. Don't be concerned if the pieces seem long; you will be trimming off the ends after you have attached the panel to the posts.

2. Assembling the Uprights

Space the uprights evenly along the two crosspieces, beginning about 5" in from one end and leaving a similar space at the other end, to allow for attaching the finished panel to the fence posts. I suggest using eight uprights, but the number may vary depending on the size of your limbs, how crooked or straight they are, and whether they have any side limbs or forked pieces. Nail each upright into place at both crosspieces. The looped arches are added after the fence is erected (see step 3 on page 39).

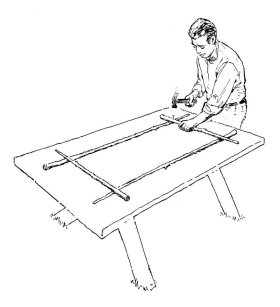

Fence Gate

The gate shown in the illustration on page 70 is 36 inches high and 32 inches wide, fitting into a 36-inch opening. It is made as a complete unit like a trellis and then cut in half to form the gate opening.

Size: 32" wide for a 36" opening

Wood Materials List			
Part Name	Number	Length	Diameter
Side uprights**	2	5'	About the size of broomstick at the base and a pencil at the top
Large inner arch**	2	4'	Slightly smaller than side uprights
Small inner arch**	2	3'	About the size of your little finger
Crosspieces	3	32"	*
Center uprights	2	36"	*
Fan pieces	2	12–15"	*

*Varies with wood used; see chapter 1 for suggestions.
**Flexible.

I. Attaching Two Crosspieces

Lay out the side uprights on your worktable. Place them 32" apart, with the bottom ends even. Position the lower crosspiece 4" from the base and nail in place. Position the upper crosspiece 18" above the lower crosspiece and nail in place. Wire all the joints securely.

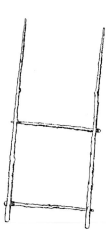

2. Forming an Arch

Bend the side uprights over toward each other to form an arch. Adjust the shape until it is visually pleasing, then wire the pieces securely to each other.

3. Adding the Third Crosspiece

Place the third crosspiece about 3" above the lower one. Nail it securely in place.

4. Attaching Inner Arches

Attach the two large inner arch pieces about 5" in from each of the outer uprights, and nail in place to the two crosspieces. Bend the two upper ends and form into an arch, wiring together. Repeat this process to form small inner arch.

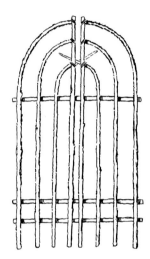

5. Attaching the Center Uprights

Place the two center uprights on the front of the trellis, about 3" apart and vertically aligned with the center of the arch. Nail them to the crosspieces and wire securely to the arch.

6. Attaching the Fan Pieces

Turn the trellis over, position the two fan pieces at approximately 45-degree angles in the arch, and wire in place.

7. Dividing the Gate

Using loppers, *cut the trellis in half* between the two center uprights. Trim the ends even with the center uprights so that the gate can be easily opened and closed.

Installing Your Panel Fence

Once you have your fence panels and gate, you are ready to set your posts and install the fence. The fence posts should be set 4 feet apart. The gateposts should be set 38 inches apart (to hold a 32-inch-wide gate). You can cut your own wooden posts (about 36 inches long and 3–4 inches in diameter) or buy posts. If you buy posts, remember that the wooden posts from the lumberyard come in 8-foot lengths. Each 8-foot post can be cut in half to make two 4-foot posts, which are adequate for this fence.

I. Setting the Posts

Measure out and stake the locations for your fence posts (4' apart) and gateposts (38" apart). Dig a hole 15" to 18" deep for each post. Set the post in the hole and firmly tamp down the soil around it. (Concrete reinforcement isn't needed for a low fence such as this.) If desired, instead of digging a hole, you can sharpen the posts and drive them with a heavy hammer (such as a small sledge hammer). Once the posts are securely in the ground, cut off any excess from the tops to leave 24" above ground. This height is for a fence and gate that is primarily decorative and is not intended for use in a high-traffic area.

2. Attaching the Fence Panels

Attach the fence panels, with the front of the panels facing forward. Nail in place, so uprights are slightly above the ground, and trim off any excess.

3. Adding the Looped Arches

Use two uprights, each 8' long and very flexible, to make the looped arches on either side of the gate. Attach the large end of each upright to the back of the gatepost and nail or wire in place. Then, arch each piece over the adjoining fence panel and bring the small end down behind the fence post, close to the lower crosspiece. Wire in place.

4. Hanging the Gate

Hang the two gate sections to the gateposts using metal pipe hanger. Attach the hanger to the posts and loop it around the gate uprights just underneath the upper and lower crosspieces (see step 3 on page 61 for full instructions).

Here-I-Am Fence

This fence makes a delightful backdrop for your favorite specimen plants. To make it, follow the instructions given on page 59 for making a basic rectangle, in this case measuring 24" high by 60" wide. Then make a small trellis (see chapters 2 and 3) with crosspieces that correspond to the fence's crosspieces and add latticework between them. Center the trellis in the fence and attach it to the back of the fence. To extend the fence, make several more panels (with or without the center trellis). Attach the panels to small posts driven into the ground with a large hammer.

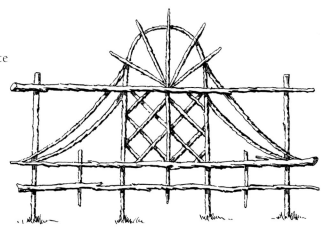

Size: 40" high at the center and 5' wide

Setting Sun

This piece can stand alone as a trellis, or it can be made into a charming fence by attaching several panels side by side. Install the panels on 36" metal or wooden posts, driven 12" deep into the ground and attach with wire. This is an easy fence to make if you have a limited amount of flexible wood, since it requires only one flexible arch. The rest is made from green or dry wood that does not need to be flexible. Note that the bottom crosspiece "supports" the arch, and the upper crosspiece is secured behind the uprights.

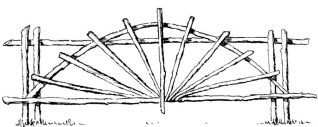

Size: 30" high and 60" wide

Golden Gate Bridge

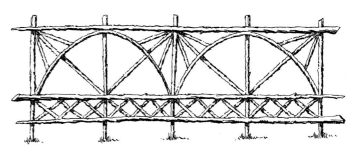

Inspired by the famous San Francisco bridge, this fence panel has a lot of bracing. Attach several of these panels side by side to make a delightful fence behind daylilies or to go along the edge of the lawn to set off a bed of perennials.

The basic rectangle for this panel is made with five uprights. The two arches are formed between the outer and middle uprights. The latticework and bracing around the arches finishes the panel.

Size: 30" high and 8' wide

Blooming Hearts

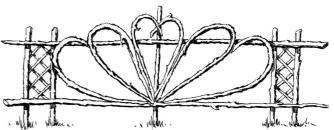

To make this fence, you need very flexible material for the hearts. Hickory, fragrant dogwood, and cedar are excellent choices for this design. If you don't have any other material, you can use grapevine for the bent pieces. Each center heart is made of two pieces, bent and wired in place. Placed behind a bed of daffodils and tulips, this trellis will send you in search of your camera at the first burst of spring bloom.

Size: Approx. 28" high and 5' wide; size varies according to materials used and needs of location.

Hearts on the Fence

Once you've built your basic rectangle, with an additional crosspiece between the upper and lower ones, line up several hearts side by side, wiring the two halves of each heart together so that the wires don't show. Drive a sharpened stake into the ground at the end of every section, then wire the section to the stakes. This design makes a nostalgic, romantic border for perennials and herbs, in either sun or shade.

Size: Approx. 28" high and 4–5' wide

Lattice and Arch

This design requires very little green, flexible wood (although if that's what's available, you can use it for the entire fence). The latticework is attached to the back between the two lower crosspieces. Note that the outer ends of the arches extend beyond the upright posts so that when the panels are attached to the posts, the arches tie the sections together visually.

Size: Approx. 28" high and 4–5' wide

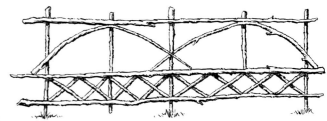

Simple Loop Border

Looped fences are easy to make and add a graceful, decorative touch to your yard or garden. The following designs require little more than plenty of flexible wood.

The universally simple arch design is easy and quick to construct. It works well around both curved and straight borders. I've seen examples of this design several times in British Columbia, and friends have seen this same little fence in places as diverse as Indonesia, Japan, and the Netherlands. It is easily constructed of bamboo, green willow, birch, oak, elm, or any sapling that is flexible.

Size: Approx. 18" high and 30" wide

I. Gathering and Preparing the Wood

Gather flexible limbs approximately 60" long with a diameter at the large end about the size of your thumb, tapering to about the size of your little finger. The quantity depends on the length of fence you plan to build.

Trim all the limbs to the same length, sharpening the ends if desired to make it easier to insert them into the ground. Limb ends will be inserted 4" into the ground to secure the border.

2. Forming the First Loop

Mark the spot on the ground where you want your fence to begin. If the soil is soft, stick the large end of one limb directly into the ground at the designated spot, pushing it in about 4". If the soil is harder, use a stake and hammer to start a hole before inserting the limb.

Bend the limb over (in the direction you want your fence to go) to form an arched loop approximately 18" high and 30" wide. Insert the smaller end of the limb into the ground.

3. Forming Additional Loops

Measure and mark a spot 8" inside your first loop. Insert the large end of a second limb at this spot, pushing it in about 4". Bend the limb over to form a second loop approximately 18" high and 30" wide, then insert the smaller end into the ground. Continue adding overlapping loops in this fashion until you have spanned the length of your fence project. It isn't necessary to tie the joints where the loops overlap, but it does add stability.

Loop Border and Band

This is a variation of the Simple Loop Border fence, with a straight band attached across the loops. This design makes for a more stable fence that will withstand a bouncing ball, leaping puppy, or light bumps with the lawn mower. However, its purpose is still more to delineate a border or direct people along a path than to act as a barrier.

The materials required are the same as for the simple loop fence, with the addition of enough straight crosspieces of wood or bamboo to run the length of the fence, each about the same diameter as the loop limbs.

To make this fence, form loops as described for the Simple Loop Border fence. Place the crosspieces where the loops intersect, overlapping the ends to make additional pieces as necessary. Wire them in place using soft, black tie wire.

Size: Approx. 18" high and 30" wide

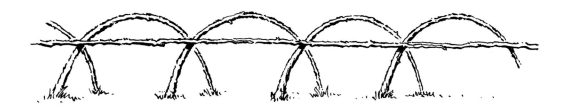

Arch and Wattle Fence

This small fence can easily be made of any flexible wood. It is a graceful addition to border plantings or boundaries. Willow, cedar, hickory, and alder are all excellent choices for this fence. The construction technique is a bit different from the trellis-based designs that are made in panels.

Size: 18" high and 30" wide

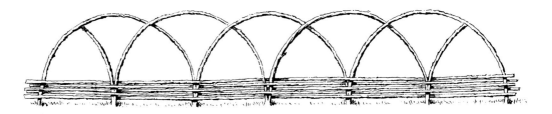

1. Gathering and Preparing the Wood

Gather 6'-long flexible limbs, about the thickness of your index finger, one for each arch of the fence. Trim all the limbs to the same length, sharpening the ends if desired to make it easier to insert them into the ground. Limb ends will be inserted approximately 4" into the ground to secure the border.

2. Forming the First Loop

Mark the spot on the ground where you want your fence to begin. Push the larger end of the first limb about 4" into the ground.

Bend the limb into an arch (in the direction you want the fence to go), making the arch about 18" high and 30" wide. Insert the opposite end into the ground approximately 4". It may help to drive small temporary stakes or pieces of limb into the ground beside each end and tie the end to the stake to hold it while you work. These can be removed once the fence has been woven together (see step 3).

Mark a spot on the ground under the center of your first arch (approximately 15" from either end) and insert the end of the next arch limb at this point. Continue making arches, overlapping them in this manner.

3. Weaving the Crosspieces

When you have the arches in place, gather a number of flexible limbs to weave in and out of the base of the arches. (The number of crosspieces, or "weavers," will vary depending on the kind of wood, length, thickness, and number of arches you have.) If limbs are too short to span the arches, overlap them to make the weavers. Beginning at ground level at one end of the fence, weave a crosspiece over and under the ends and intersecting pieces of the first arch. Wire the ends of the crosspiece to the ends of the first arch to hold it in place, if you wish. Continue weaving down the length of the fence. Working up from the ground, weave in additional crosspieces above the first ones, alternating the weave (that is, go under the piece that you previously went over and vice versa).

Continue weaving the wattle portion until it is about 8" to 10" from the ground (or until it is visually appealing). As the wood dries, it will mold to the shape you have given it. Remove the temporary stakes, if you have used them. No other finishing is required.

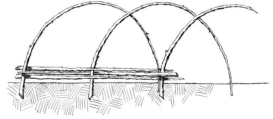

Basic Wattle Fence

The wattle fence is probably one of the oldest forms of fence construction. Basically, it involves a row of upright posts between which limbs are intertwined. The upright posts give the fence its primary strength. The "weaving" material can be any moderately flexible material, including limbs, reeds, vines, or anything else that can be woven. The resulting fence offers a barrier to animals and some privacy.

This design is for a fence with a height of up to 4 feet. If you want to build a taller fence, simply use longer uprights and plan on doing more weaving. For taller fences, I recommend setting a post in the ground every 4 feet, with about 18 inches driven into the ground. This gives the fence greater stability.

Wattle fencing can also be prepared on the ground in sections, called hurdles, then erected on posts (see page 74).

Size: Specific to needs and location

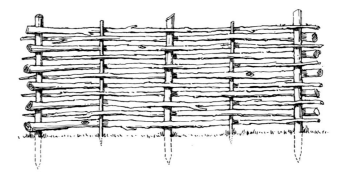

I. Preparing the Upright Posts

Measure the length of the area where you want your fence to run and divide it by 24". This gives you the approximate number of upright posts you need. Cut limbs to use as posts. These should be about 1¾" in diameter on the thicker end and the height of your finished fence plus 12". For a 24"-high fence, cut 36" posts. Don't worry about cutting these exactly to length, as you will trim off the excess when the fence is finished.

2. Driving the Upright Posts

Set out the posts along the fence line, spacing them approximately 24" apart. Drive each post about 12" into the ground.

3. Setting the Spacer Uprights

Cut enough spacer uprights to place between each pair of upright posts. The spacers should be about 24" long and slightly smaller than the posts. Push the end of a spacer into the ground halfway between the first two posts. It doesn't have to be firmly in the ground, just enough so that you can weave around it. Place the other spacers between the remaining posts.

4. Cutting the Weavers

Cut bundles of any green or nearly green wood for the weavers. These should be about the thickness of your index finger at the large end and 36" to 48" long.

5. Weaving the Wattle

Lay out one weaver at ground level with a tail of several inches of an end extending beyond the first post. Direct the weaver in front of the first post, then behind the spacer and in front of the next post. Continue weaving in and out of the uprights for the length of your fence, adding weavers by overlapping them as needed. Leave the ends extending beyond the final post.

Varying Uses

In ancient cultures, wattle fences were used to contain domestic animals near the home, as well as to keep wild animals at bay. The fence might be built 6 feet high to enclose chickens or 4 feet high to enclose pigs. A garden in danger of damage from deer might have been enclosed by an 8- or 12-foot-high fence. Wattle and daub, a method by which mud, clay, or cement is applied over the basic wood structure, was used for constructing homes.

The same rule applies for the bending pieces of the wattle fence as for trellises and gates: Use green wood that is easily flexible. If you are planning to make a wattle fence without any bent or decorative pieces, flexibility is less of a concern. You will need some pieces that are minimally flexible to use as crosspieces, or "weavers," but this is a great way to use up wood that isn't flexible enough for more complex bends, such as ash, cherry, peach, and locust. Of course, the more flexible woods, such as willow, hickory, and cedar, also work well.

To start the next row, alternate the weave, beginning behind the first post, coming in front of the spacer, and continuing on.

Continue adding rows, pushing the weavers down as you complete each row to make it firm and tight. Add rows until you reach the tops of the posts.

6. Finishing the Fence

Trim the ends extending beyond the posts to about 1" to 2". Trim off any loose overlapping pieces that are sticking out of the weave. Wire the ends of the weavers on the top row, at each post, if desired.

Building in Hurdles

Hurdles are sections of wattle fencing that can be moved or installed after being built. On a flat surface, lay out two uprights about 44" apart. Place the first weaver *on top* of the upper end of the uprights, so the weaver ends extend slightly beyond the uprights, and nail. Place another weaver at the bottom of the uprights, this time placing it *under* the uprights, and nail. Add a center upright, placing one end *on top* of the top weaver and one end *under* the bottom weaver; nail in place. Now begin weaving. Remember that when you weave, you bring the weaver over, under, and over, or under, over, and under, always doing the opposite of the previous weave. You may want to nail every third or fourth weaver in place to secure the hurdle; be sure to bend over any nails that may stick through.

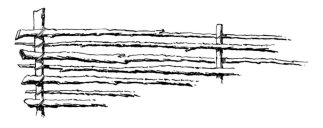

Wattle Flower Bed Border

This low fence, adapted for use as a flower bed retainer wall, works well along the edge of a patio or lawn where the flower bed is higher than the surrounding area. You could even build raised beds this way. The simple weaving pattern between the uprights is an efficient way to recycle any discarded green landscape wood trimmings from a recent pruning.

To set in the plantings, line the back of the wattle weave with black plastic and fill in with soil. The wattle border adds rustic charm to the edges of the patio, showing off the plants you grow.

Size: Can be any size desired

For uprights, you need wooden stakes about 16" long with a diameter the size of a small broom handle. These should be driven into the ground about 8". Use pieces of minimally flexible wood for weavers.

Living Fence

Another style of fence that dates back many centuries is the willow pollard, or living, fence. A pollard is a tree whose limbs have been cut back severely to the trunk to force it to maintain a short trunk and to produce multiple limbs; pollards are the *weavers* for the fence. For a living fence, the willows (the best wood for this purpose) are planted every 18 to 24 inches apart in a line. As soon as the willow has gone from being a whip to being a branched sapling (during the first or second year), all the limbs are cut back except one. In the second and third years, the limbs are cut back to the main trunk, and the cut limbs are then woven between the trunks in the same style as the weaving in the wattle fence (in and out in a basket weave).

A living fence can be made any size, depending on the time and materials you have. My example shows a 3-foot-high fence (that is trunk height, not including the bushy top). You can continue to cut off the topmost branches like a hedge or cut back only the limbs to the main trunk every other year, allowing the hedge to have a fringed top.

The goal is to produce all the weavers from the trimmings of the willows. However, there's nothing wrong with using trimmings gleaned from other trees for the weavers. Each year when the pollards are cut back, the new trimmings are added to the woven fence. This makes for a unique fence that continues to improve as it ages and grows.

To start, you can purchase willow cuttings or root your own (see Resources). Following are the steps for growing your own fence.

Size: Can be any size desired

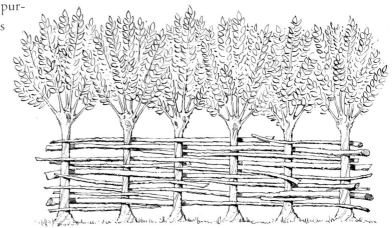

1. Preparing Willow Cuttings

Cut off limbs from a willow tree in early spring before there are leaves on the limbs. Limbs should be about the diameter of a pencil. Cut each limb into pieces about 6" to 8" long and stick the larger ends in damp peat moss or vermiculite, so that about 2" of the limb is submerged. Keep the peat moss damp. The limbs should root in about 2 weeks and can be planted when the roots are about 1" long.

2. Planting the Cuttings

Plant willow cuttings every 18" along the fence line. The cuttings will grow quickly once established. During the first year, in mid- to late summer, the cuttings will turn into whips, beginning to branch.

3. Second-Year Trimming

In the early spring of the second year, trim off the side limbs so that the willows begin to show a bare trunk. In the summer of the second year, keep the side limbs cut off, leaving just the busy top in place. As you trim off limbs, begin weaving them between the trunks of the emerging fence in a basket weave pattern.

4. Third-Year Trimming

In the late winter or very early spring of the third year, cut away all the top and side limbs, leaving only a trunk 3' high. As spring begins, the top will bush out with thick limbs. Keep weaving the cut limbs between the trunks. Your living fence is emerging with each cutting. Pack down the "weavers" a bit to make room for more.

In the summer of the third year, keep the side limbs trimmed and let the top grow.

5. Fourth-Year Trimming

In the spring of the fourth year, cut back the bushy top limbs halfway, thinning out some of the longer ones. Your living fence is now reaching maturity. Each year you should prune the tops and use the cut limbs between the trunks. A fence can be maintained this way for generations.

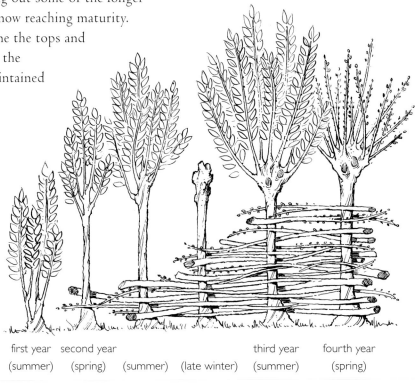

first year (summer)　second year (spring)　(summer)　(late winter)　third year (summer)　fourth year (spring)

CHAPTER 6

Arbors

When I think of an arbor, what comes to mind is the grape arbors of my childhood. These were usually simple affairs, comprising several tall posts set into the ground and connected at the top with cross-pieces. They were finished with rails or rafters across the top. Grapes were trained to grow up the posts and then over the top. It was a convenient method for growing that fruit, making it easy to prune the vines in early spring. In late summer, the bunches of grapes hung down beneath the leaves, where picking was an easy chore.

What intrigued me back then (and still does today) is how that simple structure became a room outdoors. There were no walls per se, but a line where the wall was understood to be. And there was definitely a roof — a shaded shelter where airflow kept the grapes from developing problems and where there was always a breeze in the late afternoon.

I remember my family sitting on chairs under the arbor, sipping lemonade with mint leaves, the ice cubes clinking on the glasses and the mint giving off a fresh, sooth-ing aroma. Back in those days before air-conditioning was common, the arbor was a pleasant place to spend a hot summer after-noon. Neighbor ladies would sit under the arbor, too, sewing and gossiping about the goings-on in our little town. Mothers would bring their babies and put them down on a blanket to play. Today's arbors are smaller, used less as an outdoor room than as a place to stop for a minute to sip a drink or rest on a bench; our contemporary arbors are more decorative than those of the past.

Arbor Designs

I've made numerous arbors in my gardens and have found several styles that are easy to construct and are visually pleasing. My designs use the basic trellis structure (described in chapter 2) as the foundation for the simple arbor archway. An arbor equipped with a gate makes an inviting passageway into a garden. Set inside a garden, with a trellis across the back, an arbor can offer the perfect shady setting for a bench. If you are in no hurry for your arbor to "emerge," you might want to try constructing the living arbor described on page 103. This arbor takes 2 or 3 years before it begins to look mature, but it is well worth the time and effort involved.

As with trellis construction, these projects require strong, green, flexible wood for any pieces that are bent. For the pieces that are not bent, you can use any available wood, green or dry.

Craftsman-Style Arbor

Reminiscent of the Craftsman style of architecture of the late 1800s and early 1900s, this arbor has overhead beams that extend beyond the basic structure. It is not a quick project and does require some skill. However, don't let that discourage you if you like the design. I recommend building this arbor in sections, using any kind of wood available. Build the sections as you have time, then assemble the whole thing on a sunny afternoon. There is very little bentwood in this structure, so you can use dry wood left over from storm damage or pruning projects, or even found wood such as driftwood. (For the posts, my first choice is green wood such as cedar or other wood that will last when set into the ground. If that is not available, find treated posts at the lumberyard or builder's supply store. You will also need galvanized nails that are 3 to 5 inches long.)

You might wonder why this arbor is designed to be 8 feet high. Once vines are growing on the arbor, they will hang down several inches or more; you don't want to have to duck to walk inside. The width of 6 feet allows for a wide walkway or for putting a bench on each side with a 36-inch walkway between. The arbor can provide a shady spot for conversation, picnics, or games, as well as an entryway into the garden.

Size: 8 feet high, 6 feet wide, and 4 feet deep

Wood Materials List			
Part Name	Number	Length	Diameter
Posts (either cut or bought)	4	10'	5–6"
Side beams	2	8'	6"
Crosspieces (for sides)	8	4½'	2–3"
Lattice pieces	56	20"	About the size of your index finger
Short uprights	6	Approx. 24"	1½–2"
Lower rafters	3	10'	1½–2"
Upper rafters	3	8'	1½–2"
Curved braces*	12	30"	About the size of your index finger
Fan pieces	12	28"	About the size of your index finger

*Flexible and green.

Construction Technique

Mark out the area where you want the arbor to go. Drive a stake into the ground where the first post will be set. Drive a second stake 4 feet from the first. Drive two more stakes into the ground, 6 feet from the first two, to form a rectangle.

Check to make sure the corners of your rectangle are square. You can do this easily with a piece of string. (Because the opposite sides of a rectangle are equal in length, if a rectangle is "square," the diagonal distance between corners will also be equal.) Run a piece of string diagonally from corner to corner and measure. Do the same for the other side. Adjust stake placement as needed, so diagonal distance is equal.

The stakes mark the center of each hole you will dig for the posts. Dig each hole 24 inches deep. Place a post in the center of a hole, packing stones and soil firmly around the post and filling the hole completely. Do the same for the remaining three posts. Use a level to ensure that each post is straight and square.

I. Laying Out One Side

After installing the posts, measure 8' up on each, ensuring that each post is the same length above the ground. Cut off any excess, then measure between the tops of each post. (The distance between the top of each post should equal the distance between each post at ground level.)

Place one side beam across the top of the posts on the long side of the arbor, with the ends extending an equal distance beyond both posts. Nail it in place with nails long enough to go through the beam and at least 2" into the posts (or use long deck screws).

2. Attaching the Crosspieces

Bottom crosspiece: Measure 88" below the top beam and mark the spot on both posts. Place a crosspiece between the two uprights at this spot and nail it in place; this will be the bottom crosspiece. (When the arbor is mounted in the ground, this piece will be 8" above ground level.)

Second crosspiece: Measure 28" above the bottom crosspiece, mark this spot on both posts, and attach the second crosspiece between them.

Third crosspiece: Measure 30" above the second crosspiece, mark this spot on both posts, and attach the third crosspiece between them.

Fourth crosspiece: Measure 12" above the third crosspiece, mark this spot on both posts, and attach the fourth crosspiece between them.

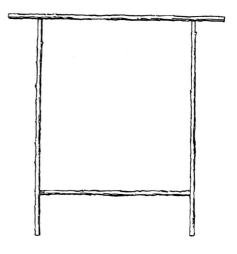

3. Attaching the Lattice Pieces

Arrange the lattice pieces in six X formations between the two upper crosspieces. Nail to the crosspieces. Arrange the remaining lattice pieces between the lower crosspieces. Nail in place.

4. Attaching the Short Uprights

Center the smaller of the short uprights in the space above the upper latticework and nail them in place. Place the two longer pieces in the space between the two lattice sections, dividing the space into thirds. Nail in place.

5. Making the Other Side

Repeat steps 1 through 4 to make the other side section.

6. Attaching the Lower Rafters

Place one of the 10' rafters across the two side beams at the front of the arbor; make sure the overhang is equal on both sides and the rafter lies directly over the joint with the post. Nail the rafter in place on both sides, making sure the nails go through the beam and well into the post below. Adjust the spacing of the top, leveling the posts if necessary.

Place another 10' rafter across the side beams at the back of the arbor, above the joint with the post, and nail it in place. Your arbor should now be fairly stable, though it will probably have a bit of a wobble or sway.

Place the remaining 10' rafter across the side beams in the middle of the arbor, so that it lies directly above the joint with the short upright (above

the upper latticework). Even out the overhang, then nail the rafter in place, driving the nail through the side beam and into the short upright on each side.

7. Attaching the Upper Rafters

Place one of the 8' rafters over the lower rafters, parallel to one side beam, adjusting the ends to be even. Nail the upper rafter to the three lower rafters. Repeat this process with another rafter placed parallel to the other side beam. Finally, add the third rafter centered between the other two, down the center of the arbor.

8. Attaching the Curved Braces

These arch pieces act as braces, helping to stabilize the structure and take out some of the sway. They should be substantial enough for that purpose (in other words, don't make them too small). To prepare the braces, prebend each one by pressing it into a slight arch. This can be done by pressing it down over the edge of a deck rail, around a post, or over the edge of a picnic table. Once you've done this, you'll have a good sense of how well each piece is going to bend, and the arch will have a bit of the desired shape before you put it in place.

Position the end of one arch piece along one of the front posts, about 18" from the top. Nail this end firmly to the post. Bend the other end to form an arch braced up against the front rafter and nail it in place. Repeat this process to attach arches to the remaining side on the front, both sides of the back opening, and along the four side corners.

9. Attaching the Fan Pieces

Nail three fan pieces behind the post at each of the four corners on the front and back. Wire them in place along the arch.

Maintaining Your Arbor

I don't use wood preservative on any of my arbors, but if you wish, you can use a garden pump sprayer to apply preservative. Do this at least 2 to 3 months before you plant anything around your arbor or during the winter when there is no vegetation. Be sure to cover nearby planting beds or evergreen plants with plastic before spraying, then soak the wood well with preservative. Also, if possible, allow the wood to cure, or dry, for 2 to 3 months before applying the preservative.

Bentwood Arbor

This is a fairly easy arbor to construct. Including cutting the wood from my land, it took me about 8 hours to build. I use this as an entryway to my garden and have a gate underneath. Clematis and cardinal climber provide the vegetation, and visitors to the garden often like to stand underneath the arbor for photos.

Before starting, review the directions for making a basic trellis in chapter 2, since this project is made much like a trellis. (*Note:* In addition to the materials listed below, you'll need four 4-foot metal posts, wire, and nails.)

Size: 6½–7' to the crosspieces, 8' to the top of the arch; the arch is 4' across at the bottom and 3' deep.

Wood Materials List			
Part Name	**Number**	**Length**	**Diameter**
Uprights*	6	16'	Approx. 1¼–1¾"
Front and back crosspieces	2	28–30"	Approx. 1–1½"
Side crosspieces	10	36"	About the size of your thumb
Side braces	8	Approx. 30"	About the size of your thumb
Rafters	4	45"	About 1"
Fan pieces (not shown)	6	Approx. 15"	About the size of your thumb

*Very flexible and strong.

1. Assembling the Uprights

Lay two of the uprights in one long line, with the small ends meeting. Overlap these ends about 2' and wire them temporarily in place, securing them in several places along the overlap. Because of the variability of wood, it is best to start with just one pair of uprights to get a feel for how your wood will bend.

2. Forming the Arches

You might want to enlist a helper for this step. Bend the joined pieces into an arch. Have one person hold the arch while the other measures to see whether it is long enough to form an 8'-high by 4'-wide arch. Adjust the overlapped ends, if needed, to obtain this height and wire securely. Run a temporary wire between the two uprights to hold the arch shape. Repeat this step with the remaining uprights to form two more arches of the same dimensions.

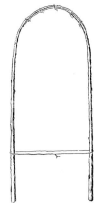

3. Setting the Front and Back Arches in the Ground

Mark the spot on the ground where you want the front arch to go and drive a 3–4' metal post there. Wire the leg of one of the arches to this post. Mark the location for the other leg of the arch, and drive a metal post at this spot.

Measure 3' back from both posts. Insert metal posts at these spots and wire the back arch legs to them.

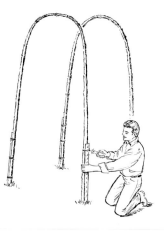

4. Attaching the Front and Back Crosspieces

Place the front crosspiece across the front arch, 6½–7' up from the ground and with the ends extending equally beyond both sides. This piece will hold the arch shape. Wire one end very securely, pull the arch together to the shape you find most pleasing, and wire the other end in place. Alternatively, if the arch shape is too sharp, use the front crosspiece to push the top of the arch apart before wiring it in place.

Repeat this step on the back arch, using the back crosspiece to form an arch that reflects the shape of the front one.

5. Positioning the Center Arch

Place one side crosspiece between the front and back arches, about 4' above ground level. Wire the two ends in place at the arches. Repeat the process to attach a crosspiece to the opposite side. Place the center arch halfway between the front and back arches, and wire it to the crosspieces.

6. Attaching the Middle Arch Crosspiece

Place one side crosspiece across the top of the center arch, 6½–7' above ground level. Wire it securely in place, adjusting the arch shape to match the other two.

7. Attaching the Rafters

The rafters tie the tops of the three arches together. Position one rafter on each side of the arch, running just above the arch crosspieces, with the ends extending equally beyond the front and back of the

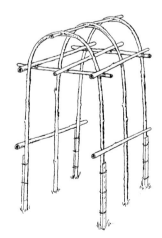

arches. Wire them securely in place. Place an additional rafter between these two and wire that in place. Position the final rafter along the top center of the arch and wire it securely in place. If you use green wood on all these parts, you will need to retighten the wire joints in about 3 weeks.

8. Adding the Fan Pieces

Add three fan pieces to the upper front "window" of the arch by securely wiring the bases of all three pieces around the lower middle rafter and the other ends to the upper arch. This fan helps stabilize the top of the arch. Repeat the process on the back arch.

9. Attaching the Remaining Side Crosspieces

Attach the remaining crosspieces along the sides of the arbor, equally spaced and wired securely in place. Use side braces to form Xs between the two lower crosspieces on each side (a total of four Xs). Step back and look at your work. Add more crosspieces if you wish to help support vines or complete the design.

Suggested Plantings

Clematis and cardinal climber both grow well on this design. You can also plant trumpet creeper and let it grow (with lots of trimming) to create a living arbor over the structure.

Easy-Living Arbor

There are many methods for making a living arbor. I spotted this design in a historic district of Philadelphia and wanted to make one myself. The arbor is very simple, does not require green wood, and can be made in a day. To look its best, however, it needs semiannual pruning and 3 or 4 years of growth to begin to look mature.

Size: About 8½' high, 8' wide, and 2½–3' deep

Materials List			
Part Name	Number	Length	Diameter
Young trees	4	6–8'	
Metal reinforcing rod	2	21'	½"
Piece of wire	1	About 5" long	
Jute twine or plastic nursery ties (don't use wire)			
Bench			

Choosing Trees

Your choice will be determined primarily by where you live, but here are some basic guidelines:

- Get four trees similar in size and shape.

- Choose "balled and burlapped" trees (i.e., field-grown trees that are dug and wrapped with burlap, keeping the roots intact) or trees grown in large nursery pots (a 6–8' tree should be in a 5-, 8-, or 10-gallon nursery pot).

- For rapid fill-in, choose trees that have side branches, not just a single whip.

- Choose trees with healthy, firm trunks; single-trunk trees are better than multiple trunks or trunks that branch into a V close to the ground.

1. Planting the Trees

Mark out a 8 × 2½–3' rectangle on the ground where you want your arbor to grow. Plant a tree at each of the four corners. Be sure to water your new trees each week and give them good care just as you would other new plantings.

2. Placing the Reinforcing Rods

Place one of the reinforcing rods next to one of the trees and push it into the ground about 12". Bend the top of the rod over toward the opposite corner. Repeat with the other reinforcing rod so that they form an X over the top of the arbor, above where the bench will go. Wire the middle of the X securely so that the two reinforcing rods are firmly attached.

3. Training the Trees

Bend one tree toward the center and tie it loosely with jute to the reinforcing rod arch. Bend another tree from the opposite direction and tie it to the rod and other treetop. Repeat with the other two trees, so that all four trees are leaning into the middle to form the arbor.

As the trees grow, keep pruning off limbs that do not conform to the arch shape. The tree limbs will fill in, making a living arch. Place a bench underneath, and you'll have a wonderful conversation spot — private, cool, and peaceful. Annual pruning can be done in early spring and again in midsummer to keep the arbor looking full. An arbor planted this way and kept pruned will grow and mature, lasting for decades.

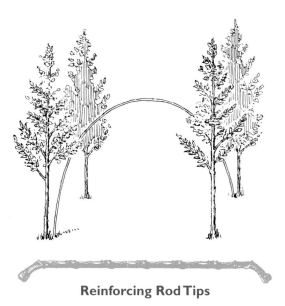

Reinforcing Rod Tips

❧ Use ½" or ⅜" reinforcing rod.

❧ Reinforcing rods come in 21' lengths. Some hardware stores may cut rods to 10½' lengths. If possible, use the full 21' piece, as it is more stable when installed.

❧ If you use two 10½' pieces, bend the arch into shape on the ground and wire together the two ends of the metal rods before installing the arch.

❧ Start the bend for the arch about 5' from the end of the rod. You will likely need someone to hold the end of the rod while you are bending it into place.

Suggested Trees and Plants

American Hophornbeam

(Ostrya virginiana)

Also known as ironwood, this is a fairly slow-growing tree (about 15 feet in 15 years), which means it will take longer to train your arbor, but it will keep within bounds and size. A small tree native to the eastern and central United States, from Nova Scotia and Minnesota south to Florida and west to Texas and Missouri, hophornbeam prefers full shade to partial shade (an advantage if you want an arbor in a shady area) and thrives in poor, dry soil. You may need to order hophornbeam from a specialty nursery or by mail.

American Wisteria

(Wisteria frutescens)

You can usually find wisteria trained into a "tree," and this is the best size to start with if using this plant in an arbor. The tree type is a vine that has been trimmed to have a trunk, about 3–4' high. The vining branches grow from that point, twisting around the reinforcing rods in interesting corkscrew shapes. Wisteria makes an excellent arbor and covers very quickly, but be prepared to prune it about every 3 weeks all season. If left unpruned, the plant will quickly grow out of bounds. As the plant ages, the trunk thickens into wonderful, twisted shapes that add visual interest. When the plant reaches 6 or 7 years of age, it should start blooming with grape-like clusters of flowers.

Apple

(Malus spp.)

Apple trees, especially the semi-dwarf varieties, accept pruning and training very well, grow fairly quickly, and make an interesting arbor. Crabapples also can be used this way and are beautiful when in full bloom. An arbor bearing fruit can be a romantic bonus to the structure. Apples tend to lose their leaves in late summer, so be prepared for less leaf coverage at that time.

Beech

(Fagus grandifolia)

A native tree that ranges from Wisconsin and Nova Scotia, south to Florida, into Tennessee, parts of Arkansas, and Texas; also available in larger nurseries.

Elm Red

(Ulmus serotina; or other Ulmus spp.)

A native tree found from Kentucky, southern Illinois, Oklahoma, Arkansas, Missouri, Alabama, Georgia, and Texas. It has shiny green leaves, is easy to train and prune, and has bright yellow leaves in the fall.

Grapevine

(Vitis spp.)

Grapes grow quickly and can be pruned and trained to the metal arbor form. This vine may begin dropping some of its leaves in late summer, but it looks attractive in any season. Having grapes to munch on while you sit on your arbor bench reading a book makes this vine even more appealing. Be prepared to prune heavily each spring, then monthly during the early summer season to keep the vines in check.

Hemlock, Eastern
(Tsuga canadensis)
This evergreen has fine, soft needles and responds well to regular pruning. Choose a tall, slender (even skinny) tree about 4 to 6 feet tall. Hemlock takes a little longer to form into the living arbor than some of the fast-growing trees, but the result is an evergreen arbor that is inviting, summer or winter.

Holly
(Ilex spp.)
Hollies stay green all season. Choose an upright variety that grows naturally into a pyramidal shape and whose leaves don't have sharp points. Ask a landscape designer at your local nursery or garden center for help in choosing an evergreen holly that does well in your area.

Japanese Privet
(Ligustrum japonicum)
Used extensively as a hedging plant, privet is tough, fast growing, and adaptable to a wide variety of soils and growing conditions. It is easily trained and accepts regular pruning very well. If you want a lush, green arbor with fast growth, which can be sculpted to your desired shape, this is an ideal plant. Buy privet as a rooted cutting or

an unbranched whip (get it as tall as possible), in any form that the nursery offers, whether potted or bare root (i.e., temporarily wrapped in plastic with peat moss for the trip home). Mail-order nurseries often offer privet very inexpensively.

Japanese Zelkova, or Saw-Leaf Zelkova
(Zelkova serrata)
You may see this tree along city streets where there used to be American elm trees. It's moderately fast growing; has dark green, shiny leaves and an upright pyramidal shape; and is somewhat resistant to air pollution. Zelkova trees are easy to train to a shape, easy to prune and have a reputation for being an excellent plant for bonsai.

Simple Walkway Arbor

The simple walkway arbor requires only a small amount of green, bendable wood for the decorative braces. Although this is a simple-appearing structure, it does require some skill in nailing the pieces together. However, do not let that prevent you from attempting this design. The only difficult part, if you have no experience doing it, is digging the holes for the four uprights. For this arbor, it is best to set the uprights into the ground about 18" to 24" deep. (We have rocks instead of soil in the Ozarks, so I usually quit at 18".) The uprights should be slightly larger around than your wrist, or about 4–6" in diameter at the base, and approximately 10' long (remember, nearly 2' goes into the ground). Don't worry about measurements too much. As with the trellises and gates, materials will vary. Use your own judgment about what looks good in your garden.

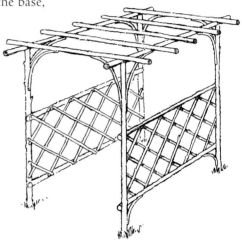

This arbor is meant for vines such as autumn clematis, small-fruited gourds, silver-lace vine, or scarlet runner beans.

Size: 8' high, 4' wide, and 6' deep

Wood Materials List			
Part Name	Number	Length	Diameter
Uprights (posts)	4	10'	Approx. 4–6"at the larger end
Side beams	2	8'	Approx. 4–6"at the larger end
Rafters	5	7'	Approx. 4–5"at the larger end
Crosspieces	4	4½'	Approx. 3–4"at the larger end
Lattice pieces	24	2–5½'	About the size of your thumb
Upper arches*	8	Approx. 3'	About the size of your thumb
Lower braces*	4	Approx. 15"	About the size of your thumb

*Green and flexible.

1. Setting the Uprights

Measure out a 4 × 6' rectangle where you want your arbor to go. Dig four holes 18" to 24" deep at the corners. Place the uprights in the holes and firmly tamp down the soil around each upright. Ensure the uprights are straight; use a level if necessary.

Measure from the ground up, level, then cut the uprights off at 8' high.

2. Attaching the Side Beams

Enlist the help of a friend for this and the next step. Place one beam on top of the two side uprights (this is the 6'-long side), so that 12" hangs over each end. Nail through the beam and into the uprights. It's important that the nails extend at least 2" into the uprights. Use two nails for each upright.

Repeat this step on the other side.

3. Attaching the Rafters

Lay the five rafters between the two side beams, placing the first and last rafters 3" from the ends of the side beams and spacing the other rafters at intervals of 20" to 24". Nail these to the tops of the side beams. Be sure all your joints are tight and the nails go at least 1½–2" into the beams below.

4. Attaching the Crosspieces

On the inside of the arbor, measure 18" from the ground on each post and mark. Position a lower crosspiece on each side between these marks. Nail the crosspiece to the back side of the posts (from inside the arbor). Trim ends flush with posts.

Measure up 3½' from the lower crosspieces on the post, mark, and position the upper crosspieces there. Nail them to the back of the posts (on the inside of the arbor). Trim ends flush with posts.

5. Attaching the Lattice Pieces

The lattice can be applied on either side of the arbor. Cut the lattice pieces for one side and nail them in place on the ends. (If you want more strength where the lattice crosses, wire some of the joints.) Repeat on the other side.

6. Forming the Upper Arches

Place the upper arches in the spaces between the uprights and the beams (or rafters) on the front, back, and both sides. It's a good idea to prebend these pieces, making sure they don't break. Securely nail one end of an arch piece about 28" down from the beam. (If it splits, your nails may be too large. Unless the splits are bad, don't worry too much about this. You could predrill holes for the nails to prevent splitting.) Bend the other end of the wood to form half of the arch. Cut off any excess and nail it in place. Repeat for all the other pieces. Use wire to secure, if necessary.

These bent sections are braces for the arbor. As they dry, the wood will stabilize, and your arbor will stiffen.

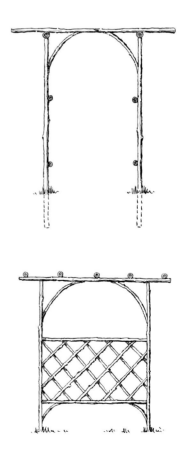

7. Forming the Lower Arches

Attach small arch braces under the bottom crosspieces at each corner, as shown in the illustration.

CHAPTER 7

Trellises Without Bentwood

lexible, green, and easily bent
wood can be found over a large
portion of North America if
you have access to rural areas, back
lots, or other timbered places.
However, many gardeners in cities,
as well as those who want to make
trellises in the more arid regions of
the United States, may not have
easy access to the flexible, newly cut
wood that I like to use. Don't
despair — there are alternatives.

Using Available Materials

I have developed several designs
using materials that are accessible
to people who live in regions that
have little hardwood to harvest. I've
included plans for using driftwood
(which includes any dry wood you

may find in the desert, on the
lakeshore, or in a city compost
area) and plans that can be easily
adapted for green or dry bamboo.
One design uses only vines, for
folks who have an excess of
grapevines or other vines. There are
designs using downed limbs from
storms, and even a design that uses
the spines from palm fronds.

If you don't have the "perfect"
green, flexible wood, use what you
have available. Just because the
wood doesn't bend, doesn't mean
that you can't build a trellis.

The unique quality that you, as
the gardener, bring to the design
and the one-of-a-kind materials you
use to build it are the elements that
give these designs life and character.
Have fun building them, and don't
be afraid to try new materials.

No-Bend Trellis

This trellis differs slightly from the basic trellis design in chapter 2 because it substitutes naturally curved pieces in place of the arched benders. Cactus wood, trimmings from orchards, and limbs downed by storms all work well for this design. Built of strong wood and nailed together well, this full-sized, sturdy trellis will hold a variety of vines.

Follow the directions for making the rectangular structure in chapter 2 (see pages 21 and 22), attaching the side and center uprights, crosspieces, and curved arch pieces. Nail securely through the material at all joints, making the basic shape. Notice that the center upright is the support for the curved arch pieces and is important for the structure.

Add any embellishments to the design using available materials. For design ideas, review the latticework, hearts, and other shapes shown in chapter 3.

Size: 7½' high and 36" wide

Wood Materials List			
Part Name	Number	Length	Diameter
Side uprights	2	4½'	Larger than a broom handle
Center upright	1	Approx. 6'	Larger than a broom handle
Crosspieces	3	3'	Larger than a broom handle
Curved arch pieces*	2	3–4'	Size of a broom handle

*Curved driftwood or the spines of 2 palm fronds with the leaflets stripped away will work here.

Pagoda Trellis

This design uses found wood. You can use dry limbs left over from a storm (which is a good way to recycle wood that might otherwise have to be sent to the landfill) or dry or green bamboo, river cane, palm frond spines, or other rigid, dry wood. Of course, you can use green wood for this design if it is available. White birch, green or dry, is an excellent choice. Note that the joints formed by the top crosspiece with the upright and "roof" piece (corner sides) are critical to supporting the very top, as they form a brace (the triangle on each side).

They should overlap, as shown in the illustration, and be nailed securely. This makes a sturdy trellis that will support moonvines, morning glories, or cardinal climber for a very attractive display at the back of a flower border.

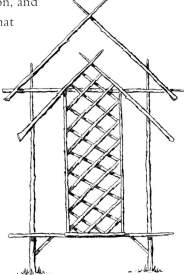

Size: 8' high and 36–40" wide.

Wood Materials List			
Part Name	Number	Length	Diameter
Crosspieces	2	4'	Approx. 1¼–1¾"
Side uprights	2	6½'	Approx. 1–1½'
Center uprights	2	4'	Approx. 1–1½'
Lower roof pieces	2	3½'	Approx. 1"
Upper roof pieces	2	4½'	Approx. 1"
Lattice pieces	18	Approx. 30"	About the size of your finger

1. Laying Out the Basic Rectangle

Lay out the basic rectangle structure as described in chapter 2, nailing the two crosspieces and two side uprights together. Be sure the uprights extend a foot or more above the upper crosspiece. (The upper roof piece must be nailed to both the upper crosspiece and the end of the upright to make a secure triangular joint. See inset taken from finished illustration.)

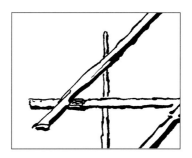

2. Attaching the Center Uprights, Roof, Lattice Pieces, and Braces

Attach the center uprights and lower and upper roof pieces, nailing each joint securely. Finish by attaching the lattice pieces between the two center uprights, trimming the pieces as needed to fit. Use the trimmings to make the two braces below the lower crosspiece.

3. Installing the Trellis

Install this trellis using one of the methods described on pages 27–28, using two metal posts driven into the ground, then securely wiring the trellis in front of the posts.

Found-Wood Trellis

This design uses trees that have limbs hanging down and curving under. Osage orange *(Maclura pomifera)* is a good example of that kind of wood, as is pin oak *(Quercus palustris)*. Several varieties of junipers grow this way as well. Often those trees' limbs are on the lower side of the branch, with very little branching on the top side of the limb. Limbs from downed trees can be used, as well as limbs salvaged from pruning. The result is a rustic and very decorative trellis that vines will climb up easily.

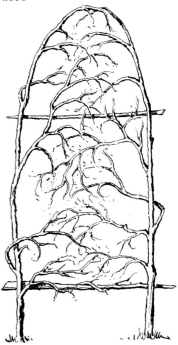

Size: Any size, depending on the size of the limbs you have; I have made this trellis as small as 30" high and as large as 8' high.

Wood Materials List		
Part Name	Number	Description
Uprights	2	Limbs that curve inward and have smaller limbs in the middle, hanging downward
Crosspieces	2	Slightly wider than the trellis (depends on materials)

1. Laying Out the Uprights

Lay the two uprights flat on the ground or other work surface. Trim off any small limbs that do not conform to the shape you have in mind and set aside. Pull the uprights close enough so that the inner limbs from both can be woven or wired together.

2. Attaching the Crosspieces

Position the lower crosspiece and nail it in place. Repeat with the top crosspiece, placing it where it is visually pleasing.

3. Wiring the Limbs Together

Bend the smaller limbs together, lacing them together or wiring them in place.

Dream Weaver

This design reminds me of a Native American dream catcher or of an upright loom. I enjoy seeing dewdrops in early morning, caught in the elaborate webs left on this trellis by garden spiders. This trellis is worth constructing just for the spiders, even if you never plant a gourd or a bean at the base. It's sturdy enough to support just about any vine and can be used in modern or naturalistic landscapes. You can use dead cactus wood, bamboo, dry cedar, pine, birch, willow, or just about anything else you have available.

Size: 7½' high and 5½' wide

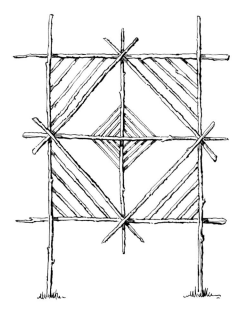

Wood Materials List			
Part Name	Number	Length	Diameter
Side uprights	2	7½'	Approx. 1½"
Crosspieces	3	5½'	Approx. 1–1½"
Center upright	1	5'	Approx. 1–1½"
Diamond frame pieces	4	4'	Approx. ¾–1"
Angle pieces	12	Approx. 3'	Approx. ¾"

1. Laying Out the Frame

Make the frame by laying out a square, with the two side uprights 5½' apart, the upper crosspiece 1' from the top, and the lower crosspiece 2' from the bottom. (Placing the lower crosspiece this high allows much of the design to show even when plants are growing up the trellis.) Using nails that are long enough to go all the way through the crosspiece and most of the way through the upright, nail the crosspieces securely in place. Nail the center upright and center crosspiece in place.

2. Forming the Large Diamond and Center Web

Lay out the diamond frame pieces between the center crosspiece and center upright, with the ends extending equally over both pieces. Nail them in place. Attach the angle pieces, beginning with the longest pieces and working toward the corners, trimming the pieces as needed to fit. Save the trim pieces and use them to make the center web.

3. Finishing and Installing the Trellis

Trim off any ends that look too long. Install the trellis using two 4' metal posts wired to the uprights.

Vine Trellis

I gather vines along the lakeshore where I live to make this design. Sometimes I use rattan vine (*Berchemia scandens*), but I also have used rose canes, small grapevines, wisteria, bittersweet, and many other plants. The kind of vine isn't important, just the fact that the vines are flexible and several can be twisted together to make a sturdy structure. The result is a charming trellis that appears delicate but is strong enough to support small vines. It looks just as good indoors in a planter as it does outdoors in the herb garden. You can make it any size you want.

Size: 36" high and 16" wide

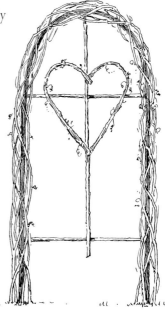

Wood Materials List			
Part Name	Number	Length	Diameter
Outside frame*	Enough for frame about 8½'		
Crosspieces	2	18"	About the size of your little finger
Center upright	1	28"	About the size of your little finger
Decorative pieces*	Additional small vines		

*Flexible vines.

1. Forming the Frame

Begin twisting the vines for the frame together, somewhat like a loose rope, adding more as you work vines until you have a "rope" about 3" in diameter (or about as large as your wrist) and $8\frac{1}{2}'$ long. Bend the twisted vines in half in the shape of the trellis. Temporarily wire or tie the ends in position. Any loose vines can be worked back in as you finish the trellis.

You can also wrap multiple vines around a small, lightweight trellis frame (see pages 20–21), adding more vines for bulk and texture.

2. Attaching the Crosspieces and Upright

Add the bottom crosspiece 10" from the bottom of the trellis and wire it in place. Position the upper crosspiece 12" from top of arch and wire it in place.

Attach the center upright, nailing or wiring it to the two crosspieces, letting the upper end extend behind the arch. Wire it to the arch as well. Trim off the vines as needed to make the trellis even on the bottom. Trim off the ends of the crosspieces if they stick out too far.

3. Adding the Decorative Pieces

Use the smaller pieces of vine to make a heart or other shapes, twisting them into rope-like pieces. Attach the pieces to the trellis using wire concealed on the back side.

Grapevine Trellis

As you probably remember from chapter 1, I strongly discourage the use of grapevines in most of my trellis projects because it is hard to control the shape. However, I saw a trellis made almost entirely of grapevines at a tourist shop in the Ozarks and was very impressed with how it looked in a garden setting. If you have large grapevines that you intend to prune back, this design is an excellent way to use up the larger trimmings. The frame is made from one large grapevine, cut green and bent into a loop. Smaller grapevine trimmings are used to lace the piece together at the bottom, where the two ends cross. The weaving in the center can be done with willow, ash, oak, or any other wood you have available, green or dry.

Size: 8' high and 38" wide

Wood Materials List			
Part Name	Number	Length	Diameter
Frame*	1	Approx. 20'	2½–3"
Bottom lacing**	—	Approx. 5'	
Crosspieces	7 (or more)	Approx. 45"	Size of finger
Center upright	1	25–30"	Size of finger

*Large grapevine.
**Green, flexible grapevine.

1. Forming the Frame

Bend the grapevine for the frame into a large loop, with the two ends crossing approximately 2' from the ground. Tie in place temporarily with string or wire. Weave the vine for the bottom lacing in and out of the uprights just above where they cross, using a simple basket weave pattern or any tying technique you are comfortable with.

2. Attaching the Crosspieces

Pull the upper part of the loop into the shape you want by weaving the crosspieces over and under the loop sides and the center upright. Wire or nail the ends of every other crosspiece to hold the shape.

3. Installing the Trellis

Install this trellis against a wall or fence rather than on posts. It is especially beautiful with 'Heavenly Blue' morning glories growing up the sides, although I can imagine training ivy or perennial sweet peas up and around the loop.

Tower Trellis

This design is so simple that it can be built in minutes if you have the material on hand. It gives height to any perennial or herb garden setting. I like it with nasturtiums or clematis — any vine that is slender and somewhat delicate, showing off the flowers and the trellis. And like the previous design, this one also uses grapevines for part of the structure.

Size: 5' high and 28–30" wide

Wood Materials List			
Part Name	Number	Length	Diameter
Uprights	4	Approx. 6'	Approx. 1½–2"
Wrapping vine*	I	Approx. 16'	Larger than your thumb at the larger end, tapering to the size of your little finger at the small end

*Grapevine.

1. Assembling the Uprights

Lay the four uprights side by side, ends even on one end at the bottom. Tie them together by wrapping a piece of wire about 8–10" from the top, making it snug but not tight.

2. Wrapping the Grapevine

Stand the trellis up, spreading out the bottom ends like a tepee. Push the bottom ends into the ground slightly. Starting with the small end of the grapevine, wrap it around the place you have wired, tucking it inside to hide the end. Continue wrapping it around in a looser ribbon, moving toward the bottom. If you choose, wire the vine to the upright occasionally to secure it in place. That's all that is required for this simple but decorative trellis. It can stay in place for many seasons, or be moved to other locations with ease.

Elegant Bamboo Tower

His Royal Highness, Prince Charles, has one of these stunning plant towers in his gardens at Hightower, his estate in Gloucestershire, England. His is made from willow, but this design is easily adapted to other kinds of wood. I like the look of bamboo for the uprights, with weeping willow for the circular weaving. To make this trellis, you must learn to make a basket weave (a simple twist of two "weavers" around an upright), but other than that, it is a pretty simple trellis to build.

Size: 5' high and 28–30" wide at base

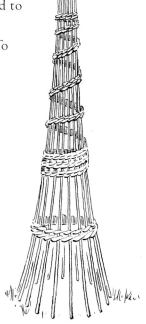

Wood Materials List			
Part Name	Number	Length	Diameter
Uprights*	15 or 17	6'	½–¾"
Weavers**	Approx. 18 to 24	6–8'	Slightly smaller than a pencil

*Slightly flexible and fairly straight
**Weeping willow limbs or other very flexible vines

1. Setting the Uprights in the Ground

To build this trellis, mark off a circle about 28–30" in diameter on the ground where the trellis will go. Insert the ends of the uprights into the soil along the circle, placing them at approximately even intervals. Make sure the uprights are about 4" in the ground, enough to be secure while you weave.

2. Adding the Weavers

Take the smaller ends of two weavers and start at the upper end of one of the uprights. Tie the ends in place with string if you wish. Go around one upright, twist the willow, then go around the next upright. As you proceed, space the uprights with your weaving so that there is about an inch between the ends. Weave this way — twisting around one upright, then twisting around the next — until you have gone around the upper end at least twice.

Using the same twist-and-weave pattern, begin a loose spiral pattern down the slope of the trellis until you are about halfway down. Add new weavers as needed, overlapping the ends. These will dry in place once the structure is completed.

At the center, continue weaving for four or five rows around the trellis, letting the weaving widen out toward the bottom. Then continue weaving downward in a spiral leaving another open space, then weave three more rounds about 12" below the center. Tuck the ends of the willow weavers inside the weaving to hide them, and the trellis is finished.

This trellis is stunning with or without vines, but if you choose to use vines, I would suggest very delicate plants that will not hide the structure itself.

Just Plain Lattice

This versatile design can serve as a trellis or a fence. It doesn't require anything special in the way of materials. In fact, it can be made from just about any wood you can find, green or dry. Make several panels and lay them on edge, installing them on short stakes for an attractive border fence. Or install one panel upright against a wall for a quiet, functional trellis that will not detract from other designs around it. It can also act as a screen next to a patio. To make this trellis more attractive, use a trim piece on top to cover the cut ends of the wood, after you have applied the lattice. Nail it in place over the ends of the lattice, using a minimum number of nails.

Size: 5½' long and 24" wide

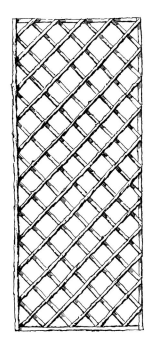

Wood Materials List			
Part Name	Number	Length	Diameter
Uprights	2	5½'	About the size of your thumb
Crosspieces	2	2'	About the size of your thumb
Lattice pieces	28	2–4'	About the size of your little finger
Trim pieces for width	2		About the size of your little finger
Trim pieces for length	2		About the size of your little finger

1. Laying Out the Frame

Lay out the uprights and crosspieces in the shape shown in the illustration and nail in place.

2. Attaching the Lattice and Trim

Attach and nail all the lattice pieces, going in one direction first and spacing them about 3" apart. Trim the pieces as needed to fit. Then place and nail the lattice going in the opposite direction. Trim off any excess. Place the trim piece over the top and bottom edges to cover the nails and ends of the lattice. Nail in place. Repeat on the two long sides.

CHAPTER 8

Selecting Plants for Your Bentwood Structures

U ltimate enjoyment of the decorative bentwood trellis, fence, or arbor you have created comes when placing it in your garden and surrounding it with vining plants. Annuals, perennials, bloomers, fruit producers, and herbs will provide beautiful accents for your bentwood.

Suggested Vining Plants

Following are descriptions of attractive vining plants for your bentwood structures. Review the growing conditions for each to learn what will work best in your area. This is not a comprehensive list, but it should give you a good starting point for making your selections.

Rating the Plants

The plants marked with an asterisk are the ones I highly recommend. Read each description carefully to learn the plant's growing requirements and habits. You will note that I've also included several plants that can be used with caution. These include plants with "bad habits," such as sprouting from the roots, which need to be monitored and controlled so that they don't take over your garden.

Annuals

Annual vines offer quick cover for a trellis. Many annuals generally require less overall pruning than perennials — a definite plus during the lazy days of summer.

Balloon Vine

(Cardiospermum halicacabum)

Also known as love-in-a-puff because of the unusual little pods that look like tiny green pumpkins. The pods contain black seeds that are marked with a heart-shaped design.

- **Growing conditions:** Does best in hot weather, full to partial sun, and average soil.

- **Height:** Climbs 6 to10 feet by tendrils.

- **Propagation:** Propagate from seed in early spring, planting outside after the last frost.

Black-eyed Susan Vine

(Thunbergia alata)

Produces cheery flowers in yellow, orange, or white, all with dark centers. Used in hanging baskets, in window boxes, and on small (3- to 5-foot) trellises.

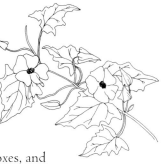

- **Growing conditions:** Partial sun, loose fertile soil.

- **Height:** 4 to 6 feet.

- **Propagation:** Propagate from seed.

Canary Vine

(Tropaeolum peregrinum)

Large, deeply lobed leaves with bright yellow, feathery flowers.

- **Growing conditions:** Grows well in full sun, in acid or alkaline soils. It prefers cool areas. In hotter climates, be sure to give it plenty of water, add some mulch, and plant other annuals around the base to keep the roots cool. I've had trouble growing this pretty little vine, probably due to our hot and somewhat dry summers. Even with mulch and regular watering, the plant has performed poorly for me, although other gardeners have reported better results.

- **Height:** Grows 8 to 10 feet and is excellent on the average-sized trellis.

- **Propagation:** Propagate from seed in spring, after the danger of frost has passed.

*Cardinal Climber

(Quamoclit pennata; also listed in some sources as Ipomoea × multifida or Ipomoea Quamoclit)

Other names for this annual vine are cypress vine and starglory. The fern-like leaves and profusion of small red flowers make this an excellent vine for the trellis. This is one of my favorite vines for showing off a trellis without concealing it with excessive foliage.

- **Growing conditions:** The plant grows and covers quickly, making it especially good for arbors, large trellises, and arches in the garden. Flowering is continuous from midsummer until frost.

- **Height:** Grows up to 20 feet but can be kept sheared to a much smaller size.

- **Propagation:** Propagate from seed. In Zone 6 or warmer, it is likely to self-propagate from the previous year's seed, although it does not often become a troublesome weed.

Cathedral Bells

(Cobaea scandens)

Also called cup-and-saucer vine. Fast growing with bell-shaped flowers that begin as pale green, then turn violet or deep blue as they mature.

- *Growing conditions:* Average soil and sun.

- *Height:* Grows 20 to 30 feet if left untrimmed. Best on arbors or large trellises.

- *Propagation:* Propagate from seed indoors or from potted plants from the garden center. Scrub the seeds briefly with sandpaper or on a sidewalk before planting (called scarifying) to help germination.

Exotic Love

(Mina lobata)

Blooms late summer into fall with long spikes of flowers that start out as red, then turn orange, yellow, and white, with all the colors appearing on the vine at one time, making for a tropical-looking display.

- *Growing conditions:* Vines do best in poor soil.

- *Height:* Grows 12 to 15 feet.

- *Propagation:* Propagate from seed.

Gourd

(Lagenaria spp.)

The small-fruited varieties are especially nice on large garden trellises and arches. They grow quickly, and the profusion of yellow or white flowers adds interest. The fruits that follow give you a nice display as the garden season draws to a close. The only disadvantage might be that the flowers attract bees (although I consider this an advantage). If you are allergic to bee stings, plant gourds at the back of the garden instead of over a garden bench. Just remember, it's the bees that pollinate the flowers to make the gourds!

- *Growing conditions:* Requires full sun and moderately fertile soil. Grows in any zone.

- *Height:* Varying sizes, depending on the variety used. Most small-fruited gourds will grow 12 to 20 feet.

- *Propagation:* Propagate from seed.

*Hyacinth Bean

(Dolichos lablab)

An attractive vine producing magenta flowers followed by pretty purple, edible pods. Vines can get heavy, so make sure you have a sturdy trellis or prune as needed. Excellent on large trellises, arches, arbors, and gazebos.

- *Growing conditions:* Likes regular moisture and good drainage. Can be trimmed to size, but excessive pruning will eliminate some of the flowering that makes this vine so desirable.

- *Height:* Grows 10 to 20 feet.

- *Propagation:* Propagate from seed indoors.

*Moonvine

(Ipomoea alba)

What a delightful vine for evenings in the garden! The flowers unfold in late afternoon, releasing a delicious fragrance that attracts interesting nocturnal moths. The spent blossoms curl and twist in an interesting way that adds more interest to this outstanding vine. Heart-shaped leaves and robust seedpods are other features that recommend this plant for the arbor or large trellis. Plant moonvine and blue morning glories together for a pleasant color mix, offering you night and morning blooms.

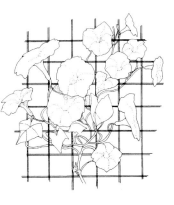

- **Growing conditions:** Blooms best when grown in poor soil that stays a bit dry.

- **Height:** Grows easily 12 to 18 feet.

- **Propagation:** Moonvine will come up better if the seeds are nicked or scratched before planting. I lay a few of them on a rock or sidewalk and use my gloved hand to scrub them on the surface. Then I place the seeds in little pots that have been filled with potting soil and start them about 2 weeks before our last frost date, getting them ready to plant outside. In climates warmer than my Zone 6, moonvine will often self-seed and come up on its own. You can then transplant it to your chosen location near your arbor or large trellis.

*Morning Glory

(*Ipomoea purpurea*)
Old-fashioned varieties such as 'Heavenly Blue', 'Scarlet O'Hara', and 'Pearly Gates' are perfect annuals for the rustic trellis. Plant this one where you can enjoy the lovely morning flowering. The only objections I have are that morning glories readily cross colors when two colors are planted together, and they spread their seeds everywhere, resulting in a bit of weeding each spring. Mulching your garden with straw or other organic mulch will help eliminate the weed problem.

- **Growing conditions:** Needs morning sun.

- **Height:** Grows to 15 feet.

- **Propagation:** Propagate from seed, but don't save seeds from year to year unless you enjoy the crossed-up colors the vine can produce. Goes from seed to flower in just weeks.

*Nasturtium

(*Tropaeolum majus*)
Those nasturtiums marked "trailing" on the seed packet can be trained up a trellis, although they do not always lift themselves up on their own, nor do they have tendrils as some vines do. This is a lightweight, colorful vine that can look stunning on small to medium-sized trellises. Nasturtium vines offer the added bonus of colorful, edible flowers that dress up salads.

- **Growing conditions:** Easily grown in average soil. I use nasturtiums to test my soil fertility, since this plant blooms best in poorer soils. If you get mostly leaves and few flowers, your soil has a high nitrogen content.

- **Height:** Grows up to 8 feet and requires some tying to keep on the trellis. You will be rewarded with lush foliage and a profusion of yellow, orange, and red flowers.

- **Propagation:** Propagate from seed in spring, after the danger of frost has passed.

*Snapdragon, Climbing

(*Asarina scandens* and *Asarina Barclaiana*)
Also called chickabiddy. Climbing snapdragon is a native of Mexico. The single white, pink, or deep blue flowers dangle like upside-down snapdragons, providing a floral display that runs almost non-stop from early summer to late fall. Used in hanging baskets, in window boxes, and on medium-sized trellises.

- **Growing conditions:** Fertile to average soil, full to partial sun. Grows well in large containers, too.

- **Height:** Trails (rather than climbs, so it will need a little bit of training to the trellis) 4 to 8 feet.

- **Propagation:** Propagate from seed indoors.

*Spinach, Vining

(*Basella alba* and *Basella alba.* 'Rubra')
Also known as Malabar spinach or Indian spinach, this is an excellent trellis vine. The attractive, glossy, heart-shaped leaves are thick and fleshy.

- **Growing conditions:** Vining spinach is a tough plant, taking poor soil and full sun. It grows easily up a trellis or archway, covering the area by midsummer and looking beautiful until frost. Pruning makes it easy to keep this vine in shape, and you can cook and eat the leaves.

- **Height:** Grows 15 to 30 feet if not pruned, but it responds well to trimming and can be kept to a smaller size.

- **Propagation:** Propagate by seed after the last spring frost. In my garden, it reseeds itself but has never become weedy.

Sweet Pea, Annual

(*Lathyrus odoratus*)
Looks nice on small to medium-sized trellises, but the plant and flowers will disappear as soon as the hot weather arrives. Sweet peas add a splash of early color to the garden.

- **Growing conditions:** Best grown in cooler weather or cooler climates.

- **Height:** Can grow up to 6 feet, but it doesn't really climb as much as it pulls itself up with tendrils. Generally shorter in most gardens.

- **Propagation:** Propagate from seed in very early spring (mid-February in the Ozarks).

Sweet-Potato Vine

(*Ipomoea batatas* 'Blackie' and others)
Sweet potatoes can be trained to a trellis with some encouragement. They are usually grown as a

vegetable, left trailing on top of the soil. 'Blackie' is especially nice because of its dark maroon leaves mixed in with dark green ones deeper in the plant where the sun doesn't reach. Will need some help growing upward on the trellis, but it is easily tied and trained.

- **Growing conditions:** Loose soil, full sun.

- **Height:** Grows 6 to 10 feet and can easily be trimmed to a smaller size.

- **Propagation:** Propagate from plant or slips taken from the tuber and rooted in water.

Perennials

Perennial vines have the advantage of being permanent, unlike annuals that must be replanted each year. Often, the woody vines of perennials can be left in place to add visual interest to a trellis or arbor. Some perennials require regular pruning to be kept in check. Most of the perennials listed here are best for arbors and larger structures.

Akebia
(*Akebia quintata*)
Also called five-leaf akebia or chocolate vine, this semi-evergreen vine is an excellent choice for shade or sun. Native to Japan, China, and Korea, akebia flowers in early summer at night, giving off an intense fragrance. Flowers are sometimes followed by purple seedpods later in the season (which are listed as "edible but insipid").

- **Growing conditions:** Akebia thrives in sun and well-drained soil. When growing up an arbor or gazebo, the vine requires some tying at intervals to keep it on the structure. Hardy in Zones 7 through 10, possibly into Zone 6.

- **Height:** Grows 12 to 15 feet. Can be pruned to keep it smaller.

- **Propagation:** Propagate from seed, root divisions, or green wood cuttings.

*Bougainvillea
(*Bougainvillea* spp.)
Bougainvillea is a southern vine, grown as a perennial in Zones 9 and 10 and as an annual farther north. The flowers are hardly noticeable, but the bracts that surround them make this vine one of the most colorful in the garden. It can become top-heavy, so it is best pruned to keep it smaller for a trellis. Also used in hanging baskets.

- **Growing conditions:** Grows in full sun to partial shade. Likes a warm climate and loamy soil containing compost.

- **Height:** Grows 20 to 30 feet, although it can be kept smaller with pruning. May require some encouragement (tying) to help it upward on the garden trellis or arch, as it climbs by way of hooked thorns rather than tendrils.

- **Propagation:** Propagate from cuttings or potted plants.

*Clematis
(*Clematis* spp.)
This family of vines offers lots of options for the trellis or arbor. Some well-known clematis varieties,

such as the large-flowered 'General Sikorski' and 'Miss Bateman', are robust climbers and can be used on a large trellis or small arch. Probably the best-known variety, *Clematis × jackmanii,* is a medium-sized vine with pleasing purple flowers that combine well with red climbing roses for spectacular color on a large trellis, arbor, or arch. I highlight some of the more popular smaller varieties below.

- **Growing conditions:** Average garden soil with some compost is sufficient. Clematis does best where its roots are shaded by other, shorter plants, such as small shrubs or medium-sized annuals. Morning sun and afternoon shade produce the best color on some varieties. All garden clematis varieties like moderate to full sun, unless otherwise noted.

- **Height:** Grows 6 to 20 feet, depending on the variety.

- **Propagation:** Best grown from potted plant or rooted cutting, although even the larger-flowered kinds can be grown from seed (with some determination and quite a bit of luck).

Clematis pitcheri

C. pitcheri, or leatherflower, can be found throughout the Ozarks and in Indiana, Iowa, Nebraska, Tennessee, Arkansas, Missouri, Oklahoma, and Texas. The small vines have attractive little bell-like flowers followed by feathery seeds.

- **Growing conditions:** Grows in full sun or partial shade; tolerates poor, rocky, or average soil.

- **Height:** Grows to 6 feet. Best for a medium-sized trellis.

- **Propagation:** Leatherflower is one of the easier clematis to propagate from seed. Put ripe seeds in the freezer for 2 weeks, then lay them on top of potting soil, press them down into the soil or lightly cover, and keep moist. Or spread the seeds in garden soil in fall, mark with a plant marker, and let them come up the following year.

*Clematis macropetala

C. macropetala is another especially good clematis for the arch or arbor. Masses of purple to deep blue semi-double flowers in early spring give a stunning display.

- **Growing conditions:** Grows in full sun, average soil.

- **Height:** Grows 8 to 12 feet.

- **Propagation:** Propagate from potted plants or rooted cuttings from a nursery.

Clematis virginiana

C. virginiana, commonly called virgin's bower, is found in the wild in thickets and woodland edges from Nova Scotia to Georgia, Louisiana to Kansas, and north into Canada. Best used on a strong arch, arched tunnel, or arbor. I've used this plant on a trellis to screen the afternoon sun on a small porch, and the pleasantly fragrant clusters of small white flowers make it even more desirable. Virgin's bower can grow top-heavy without pruning. The trunk of the plant will grow to 2 inches in diameter in about 5 years. Prune back one-third to one-half in winter or early spring to encourage bloom.

- **Growing conditions:** Will tolerate a wide range of soils and zones.

- **Height:** Grows to 25 feet and can be trimmed to keep it in shape.

- **Propagation:** Propagate from root divisions, hard wood cuttings, or seed.

*Dutchman's-pipe

(Aristolochia tomentosa)

A highly recommended and seldom-used vine. I find this native plant growing along the White River in Arkansas, where it climbs upward through the shade to display its old-fashioned, pipe-shaped blossoms in heavily filtered sunshine. Some pruning will show off the yellow to white pipe-shaped flowers, which are often hidden by the large heart-shaped leaves.

- **Growing conditions:** Found growing in the wild from Florida to Texas and north to the Carolinas, Indiana, Illinois, Missouri, Arkansas, and Kansas, Dutchman's-pipe also is available through mail-order nurseries. Other aristolochias that go by the name of Dutchman's-pipe are *Aristolochia durior* (which is native to the eastern United States), *Aristolochia manshuriensis,* and *Aristolochia grandiflora,* each with different flower sizes. Check to see which varieties are available in your area. Once established, Dutchman's-pipe is easy to grow and is adaptable to partial sun or full shade. A friend gave me a start of the one I have growing on my arbor, where it gets morning sun and has its roots in the moist, cool soil where I also grow obedience plant *(Physostegia virginiana),* lily of the valley, wild ginger, and ferns.

- **Height:** Grows up to 30 feet under optimum conditions, although the average size is 12 to 15 feet. It can easily be kept to that size by light pruning.

- **Propagation:** Propagate from seed, root divisions, or potted plants from a nursery.

Grape

(Vitis spp.)

Generally speaking, grapevines aren't the best for growing on small arbors or trellises. They have a tendency to get too large and heavy. However, grapes are a versatile family of plants and can be used on a sturdy arbor or gazebo. Find out which grapes, wild or cultivated, do best in your area.

The Wild Grape

I gathered wild grapes in the fall one year from the vines along the road to my house. I boiled the grapes and processed the juice, making it into delicious grape jelly for my winter breakfasts. I threw the seeds in the compost pile, assuming the light boiling damaged potential germination. Surprisingly, I found lots of little grape seedlings in the compost the following spring. I transplanted those seedlings to an arbor I had made from cedar poles, and they covered it by the second year. I also planted one of the seedlings beneath my bell tower, and the vines climbed upward 40 feet, softening the lines of the tower.

To maintain the grapevines on both the arbor and the tower, I trim everything back to a main stem in January or February. (The time of year is important so as not to damage the vines.) New growth produces blooms and grapes.

- **Growing conditions:** Grapes are grown throughout the United States. Zones vary depending on the variety.

- **Height:** Grows 20 to 40 feet, depending on variety.

- **Propagation:** Propagate from native seed or from plants bought bare-root or potted from a nursery.

Honeysuckle

(Lonicera sempervirens)
This vine, with its 2-inch-long, red, trumpet-shaped blossoms, is very attractive for arbors and arches. It will take hard pruning and in fact blooms better if pruned back by at least one-third in very early spring. It can become top-heavy unless your arbor is strong (and your will to prune is equally so). Once, when my honeysuckle had gotten out of hand, growing beyond the arbor and onto the roof of my herb shop, I simply walked along the roof with my power weed trimmer and pruned back the vine. I do not recommend anyone doing that because of the danger of walking off the roof, but I include my experience here to make the point that this particular honeysuckle is one very tough plant that can be ignored and still brought back into shape (although not as neatly as hand-pruning would accomplish). Not as fragrant as some of the other honeysuckles, but a pretty bloomer with nice foliage.

- **Growing conditions:** Hardy in Zones 5 through 9.

- **Height:** Grows up to 30 feet.

- **Propagation:** Propagate from cuttings or root divisions.

Honeysuckle, Everblooming

(Lonicera heckrottii)
Often trained as a bush or as a trailing vine to spill out over a wall or small structure, this honeysuckle can be trained upward on a substantial trellis or arbor and benefits from early support. Very fragrant with red and yellow flowers.

- **Growing conditions:** Prefers rich, well-drained soil, although the plant will tolerate much poorer, drier soils. Likes full sun to partial shade. Hardy in Zones 5 through 9.

- **Height:** Grows up to 30 feet. Trim to keep it from getting top-heavy.

- **Propagation:** Propagate from seed, rooted cuttings, root divisions, or potted plants from a nursery.

*Honeysuckle, Dropmore

(Lonicera × brownii 'Dropmore Scarlet')
An especially good bloomer and one of the hardiest of the vining honeysuckles. Named by Dr. Frank Skinner, who developed it in Dropmore, Manitoba.

- **Growing conditions:** Blooms from June until frost in Minnesota and is quite hardy.

- **Height:** Grows 20 to 30 feet.

- **Propagation:** Propagate from rooted cuttings, root divisions, or potted plants from a nursery.

Honeysuckle, Japanese

(Lonicera japonica)

An evergreen vine with yellow and white flowers, this rampant grower has escaped cultivation when planted along highways to prevent erosion. Not recommended for trellises or arbors because of its aggressive behavior.

- *Growing conditions:* Grows in a wide variety of soils and climates.

- *Height:* Grows 20 to 40 feet.

- *Propagation:* Propagate from seed, rooted cuttings, or root divisions.

*Honeysuckle, Yellow

(Lonicera flava)

Native to the Ozarks and occasionally available in nurseries in other areas, this is one of the best honeysuckles for the average-sized trellis located in full to partial shade. In its natural setting, yellow honeysuckle (not to be confused with Japanese honeysuckle, which has yellow and white flowers and is a non-native, evergreen vine) is a small vine, not invasive and neat in habit. It grows in rocky woods, on ledges, and along streams in Illinois, Missouri, Arkansas, Texas, and Oklahoma.

Yellow honeysuckle is a very desirable trellis plant because of its attractive blue green leaves and striking display of brilliant orange to bright yellow flowers in spring. Like most honeysuckles, this one has red berries that the birds enjoy. A neighbor of mine grows yellow honeysuckle in a large planter next to his northeast-facing porch.

He has trained the plant up a post and keeps the top pruned into an attractive zigzag pattern on a piece of metal fence. The plant's leaves and flowers grow outward toward the light, and when it is in bloom in spring, it puts forth a stunning display of blossoms that drives the hummingbirds into a frenzy as they compete for the sweet nectar.

- *Growing conditions:* Prefers full shade to partial sun. Average soil with some compost and good drainage. Hardy in Zones 5 through 7.

- *Height:* Grows 10 to 15 feet.

- *Propagation:* Propagate from seed or cuttings.

Ivy, English

(Hedra helix)

English ivy is a robust, mostly evergreen vine that can add interest to the arch or arbor, although it's usually not recommended for the trellis. The plant takes 2 to 3 years to get established, sometimes longer depending on the climate, then requires one or two prunings per year to keep it in shape. Ivy has a tendency to cover anything it is grown on, so be prepared for it to cover up your work if you choose this plant. Unless you want a purely green, simple plant covering on your structure, it would be best to choose some other vine. Small-leaved ivies work very well for topiary work and could be an attractive trellis plant if you wanted to spend some time training them.

- **Growing conditions:** Prefers shade or partial sun and average garden soil. Can become invasive if allowed to escape into woodlands. In most conditions, it's easily controlled and pruned. Hardy in Zones 5 to 10, depending on the variety.

- **Height:** Grows up to 40 feet or more.

- **Propagation:** Propagate from cuttings rooted in peat moss.

Kiwi, Hardy

(Actinidia kolomikta)

This kiwi grows with two colors of leaves — lush green mature leaves and pink, white-tipped new growth — making the vine appear to be blooming. The actual blossoms are not noticeable but have a pleasant, if faint, fragrance. Fruits on previous season's wood.

Kiwis are large and best suited for a large arch or arbor rather than a trellis. *Actinidia polygama* has silvery foliage. *Actinidia arguta* 'Issai' is self-pollinating and produces edible fruits. (Most of the other kiwis require a male and a female plant to pollinate and produce varying amounts and sizes of edible fruits.)

- **Growing conditions:** Best grown where the plant gets morning sun and afternoon shade. Tolerant of a wide range of soils up to a pH of 7.3. Hardy in Zones 4 through 10, depending on the variety.

- **Height:** Grows 20 to 30 feet.

- **Propagation:** Propagate from rooted cuttings, potted plants, or bare-root stock from a nursery.

Jasmine, Star

(Jasminum nitidum)

Also called Confederate jasmine. This well-behaved climber is a southern plant with shiny, dark green leaves, maroon flower buds, and very fragrant white star-like flowers. It can be grown as an annual or moved inside before the first frost in more northern climates.

- **Growing conditions:** Prefers full sun to partial shade and light soil with compost and good drainage. Hardy in Zones 9 through 10.

- **Height:** Grows 10 to 20 feet.

- **Propagation:** Propagate from rooted cuttings or potted nursery stock.

*Mandevilla

(Mandevilla suaveolens) [formerly *Mandevilla laxa*]

Sometimes called Chilean jasmine, mandevilla is hardy only in Zones 9 and 10. The plant is easily grown as an annual on a trellis, arbor, or screen. It also is planted in hanging baskets. The delightful deep pink or white flowers are outstanding where the fragrance can be enjoyed. The scent reminds me of the currant jelly my mother used in vanilla-flavored jelly rolls. I find that on summer afternoons when the shade approaches my garden, I stop and smell the rosy flowers almost every day, just for a whiff of my childhood.

- **Growing conditions:** Grows in fairly rich, well-drained soil in full sun or partial shade. Deadheading (cutting off the wilted flowers before they develop seeds) keeps the flowers coming. Fertilizing well with fish emulsion during the summer produces excellent results.

- **Height:** Grows up to 20 feet, but it can be kept smaller with pruning.

- **Propagation:** Propagate from stem cuttings, rooted in peat moss or another rooting medium, or from seed in early spring. I dig my mandevilla in the fall before frost, cut back the plant to 15 inches, repot it, and move it inside for the winter. The following spring, I put the plant back in the ground next to the trellis.

Passionflower

(*Passiflora* spp.) Found from the Midwest south into Mexico and beyond. Some passifloras, especially those grown from seed assortments labeled "annual," will produce red, pink, or other color blossoms. In colder regions, these types will produce nice foliage and flowers, then die back with freezing temperatures. If you live in Zone 8, 9, or 10, those varieties are probably hardy for you.

Passiflora incarnata, which is found growing in the wild from Pennsylvania south to Florida and west to Missouri and Texas, should be used on arbors and archways with caution (see box). It's a beautiful plant with a long history of medicinal uses. (It's still used today as an ingredient in herbal sedatives found in health food stores.)

The showy purple or, rarer, white flowers bloom through midsummer, followed by egg-sized and shaped, edible, tart fruits that smell like tropical punch as they ripen and dry. The fruit is ripe when it is light tan and papery on the outside, looking sort of shriveled. I have a friend who used the fruits to flavor a custard for filling cream puffs, which he served as a very tasty dessert.

- **Growing conditions:** Tolerates sun or shade and a wide variety of soils, even dry, poor, and rocky soils.

- **Height:** Grows 10 to 15 feet. This easily trained plant can be pruned to size.

- **Propagation:** Propagate from seed or root divisions. Seeds are best started early in pots indoors, then transplanted to your trellis site.

Caution on Passionflower

Passionflower has the habit of sending out shallow roots that sprout in unexpected places in the garden or lawn. These are fairly easy to keep in check with the lawn mower, but they can be a nuisance.

Silver-lace Vine

(*Polygonum aubertii*) I chose this vine, also called mile-a-minute vine, to cover an arbor quickly a few years ago. Although I was definitely anxious to have a plant on my new arbor, I wish I had done a bit more research on this one. It's aggressive, taking off immediately. It needs some help getting up on the trellis and tends to have lots of side branches hanging down, looking for something to grasp (instead of just shooting upward like some vines). The vine has an abundance of moderately pretty white flowers all season, making it look deceptively fragile, but it is tough and requires regular trimming. I use the power weed trimmer on mine three or four times a season, chopping off the unruly side branches that will hang back down to the ground from a height of 10 feet or more.

This plant can be beautiful on a large structure, but it is too aggressive for smaller locations. It can be very useful for a difficult area where little else will grow, and it will cover an arch or arbor quickly.

- **Growing conditions:** Tolerates a wide variety of soil conditions and likes sun or partial shade. Hardy in Zones 4 through 9.

- **Height:** Grows up to 30 feet.

- **Propagation:** Propagate from stem cuttings, root divisions, or seed.

Sweet Pea, Perennial

(Lathyrus latifolius)
Rose-colored or white blossoms. The plant is widely naturalized along roadsides and fences and around old homesteads throughout the central United States. Not a good climber, the perennial sweet pea prefers to grow over a fence, cover a small bush, or hang over a wall. It can be trained up a trellis or even a small arch if you start when it is small. (When the plant gets heavy, the vines break if you try to change the direction in which it is growing.) Sweet peas can be pruned to keep in shape and must be tied to the trellis to encourage attachment.

- **Growing conditions:** Likes average soil and full sun to partial shade. A yearly application of compost in early spring will encourage bloom.

- **Height:** Grows up to 9 feet.

- **Propagation:** Propagate from seed or root divisions.

Trumpet Vine

(Campsis radicans)

This plant can be used successfully on arbors if you realize that it will require trimming a few times each year. Trumpet vine will make a living arbor with a substantial trunk that can reach up to 12 inches in diameter after several years. The drawback to trumpet vine (also called trumpet creeper, which reveals the drawback) is that it creeps by its roots and can invade the lawn.

In my own lawn, I simply mow off the sprouts that come up near the trumpet vine that grows on my archway. Hummingbirds enjoy the red or orange flowers, and children enjoy popping the unopened flower buds. When used as a plant to create a living arbor, several prunings per year will keep it trimmed and within bounds and may even eventually replace the temporary structure of the arch.

- **Growing conditions:** Prefers full sun and tolerates any soil, even poor, dry soil. Sprouting from the roots seems to be less of a problem in average to good garden soil. Hardy in Zones 4 through 9.

- **Height:** Grows 30 to 60 feet or more.

- **Propagation:** Propagate from seed, cuttings, or root divisions.

A Trumpet Vine's Ascent

Many years ago, I did landscape work for a doctor and his wife, who had built a house over the spot where a trumpet vine had been growing. The vine came up in the crawl space under the house, where they made several attempts to kill it. Roots sprouted up in flower beds on two sides of the house where they again attempted to poison the plant. It grew underground for more than 100 feet, coming up in several areas. Eventually, the homeowners followed my suggestion of erecting a large, 20-foot pole for the plant with a birdhouse on top, rather than continuing to use the herbicides. The vine went up the pole and caused no further problems beyond an occasional sprout in the flower bed near the pole.

Virginia Creeper
(Parthenocissus quinquefolia)
Also called five-leaved ivy or woodbine, this is another seemingly dainty vine to use on an arbor, large trellis, or background screen. Its good qualities include rapid cover, dark green leaves, and virtually no pests. Its negative attributes are that birds carry the little black seeds and drop them in other parts of the yard, where they sprout and attempt to climb upward. However, this vine is not nearly as invasive or hard to control as wild yam or trumpet vine, and I've used it with success. It grows naturally in the woods from Florida to Texas; north to Maine, Vermont, Quebec, New York, Ohio, Indiana, Illinois, Wisconsin, and Minnesota; and south into Mexico and Guatemala.

- **Growing conditions:** Prefers partial to full shade; does well in average to poor soil.

- **Height:** Grows up to 60 feet if left untrimmed.

- **Propagation:** Propagate from seed, root divisions, or cuttings.

Wisteria, Japanese
(Wisteria floribunda)
This plant has a tendency to wrap itself tightly around any available support and can choke a tree, or even itself, if allowed to. Be sure to provide

adequate support if planting this vine on an arbor. The arbor should be at least 10 feet tall and made of sturdy material, since the weight of the vine can be substantial. If you're using wisteria for a living arbor, several prunings a year will encourage a thicker trunk and less vining. It takes 6 to 10 years for wisteria to bloom from seed or cuttings, so be prepared to enjoy the foliage while the plant is getting established. The flowers of Japanese wisteria are usually more fragrant than those of Kentucky wisteria (see below).

At the Biltmore Estate in North Carolina, wisteria was planted in the 1890s on a heavy metal arbor. The arbor "ceiling" is about two stories above the patio area, making a spaciously pleasant shady area for afternoon entertaining. With trimming, the plant has been kept to size, and the trunks of the wisteria are as big around as a slender person!

- **Growing conditions:** Grows in average garden soil with compost added. Hardy in Zones 5 through 9.

- **Height:** Grows up to 50 feet or more.

- **Propagation:** Propagate by root divisions, cuttings, or seed.

Wisteria, Kentucky

(Wisteria macrostachya)

Wisteria can be an excellent choice for a living arbor when trained on metal supports or sturdy bentwood (which will eventually rot as the wisteria trunk becomes its own support). Remember these two caveats: (1) the vine will need several prunings each year to keep it to the size you want, and (2) be sure your arbor is high enough (at least 10 feet) to accommodate the foot-long racemes of light purple to lilac flowers that hang down through the foliage.

Wisteria, if ignored, can get out of hand. In Mississippi, for example, some homeowners who moved away from the family farm and returned after 15 years found that the one wisteria vine that had been on an arbor when they left had overtaken the lawn, house, and outbuildings, having covered most of 2 acres of their property, even some of the trees! By contrast, I have seen a 100-year-old wisteria vine in North Carolina that has been trained to an arbor and easily kept within bounds by a few simple prunings each year.

- **Growing conditions:** Grows in average garden soil, in full sun to partial shade. Fertilize with compost in early spring. Hardy in Zones 3 through 9, with the best flowering in Zones 5 through 9.

- **Height:** Grows up to 50 feet or more.

- **Propagation:** Propagate by cuttings, root divisions, or seed.

Yam, Wild

(Dioscorea villosa)

This can be found growing in the wild from Connecticut to Tennessee, Minnesota to Texas. Once used as a folk remedy for a variety of ailments (see *A Field Guide to Medicinal Plants**), synthesized products from this plant include contraceptives and treatments for Addison's disease, allergies, and premenstrual syndrome. (Never self-medicate with any plant unless you have checked with your doctor first. Wild yam is not safe to use at home.)

The plant produces an underground tuber, sometimes of substantial size, along with little "leaf tubers" at each leaf node. It's a quick grower, which is why I planted a few of the leaf tubers at the base of my cedar and bentwood gazebo the year after I built the structure. The tubers sprout quickly and grow upward at a rate of several inches a day, reaching a height of 30 feet in one season. The non-showy flowers are almost too sweetly scented, but not offensively so, and the profusion of heart-shaped leaves makes this a good cover plant if used with caution (see box). The vine has little weight and climbs easily.

- *Growing conditions:* Wild yam is not particular about soil, although it is found in wet woods in its natural state. Grows well in full sun or full shade. Hardy in Zones 4 through 9.

- *Height:* Grows quickly up to 30 feet or more. Can be pruned back.

- *Propagation:* Propagate from leaf tubers, seed, and underground tubers.

Caution on Wild Yam

The little "leaf tubers" (my description of the grape-sized tubers that grow at each leaf) drop in the fall. One plant can produce several quarts of these, which lie dormant until the spring, when they sprout into a forest of vines. Wild yam can become invasive quickly unless kept in check. I've enjoyed the vine on my gazebo, but I'm always fighting the millions of sprouting tubers that try to come up in my garden paths. Use caution when choosing this plant, because it may endear itself to your flower beds.

Other Vining Plants

There are many more vines not listed here that are worth trying on your trellis. Some are available in specialty seed catalogs; others can be found by asking your neighbors what grows best for them. Some of my most prized vines have come from visits to other people's gardens. Trading seed is a tradition among gardeners, and most are willing to trade you seed from a special plant of theirs for seed of one of yours. Use the list in this chapter as a guide for possible plants, but also try other vines that you find available in your area.

*Foster, S., Duke J. A Field Guide to Medicinal Plants: Eastern and Central North America. Boston: Houghton, 1990.

CHAPTER 9

Enjoying Your Bentwood Structures

I have two principles I try to follow when it comes to bentwood projects: (1) enjoy the process of building as much as possible, and (2) take time to enjoy the work after I have finished. After all, if it isn't going to be pleasant and enjoyable, why do it?

In this chapter, I suggest ways to get the greatest enjoyment from your bentwood projects. Some are as simple as stopping and having a cup of tea on the garden bench under your arbor or taking a photo of your work to share with someone else. Since food and beverages enhance any event, large or small, I have included some of my favorite herbal recipes.

A Meditative Retreat

A cool, green living arbor offers a very private spot for reading a book or engaging in quiet meditation. Tucked into the side of the lawn or behind the house, it doesn't require any other landscaping to enhance the space. If desired, you might add a border of short annuals, such as ageratums, marigolds, or geraniums, along the edges of the

living trees. These could even be color-coordinated with a pillow on the garden bench.

A cup of calming tea can be just the thing to bring you completely into the moment, surrounded by your arbor. You might want to take along a muffin if you plan to enjoy a favorite book while sitting under the living arbor.

Meditation Tea

This quieting tea can be made with herbs picked from your garden, or you might purchase the ingredients. You'll need 2 teaspoons of tea per cup. To dry fresh herbs, lay them in a single layer in an open basket out of the light (such as in the pantry or in the cold oven). Note: The flavor of the chamomile flowers is best when dried; the other ingredients work well whether fresh or dried.

1 tablespoon dried chamomile flowers
1 tablespoon fresh or dried lemongrass, cut into 1-inch pieces
1 tablespoon fresh or dried lemon balm leaves
2 large fresh hibiscus flowers, *petals only* (red or dark pink), or 2 tablespoons dried
2 teaspoons fresh or dried spearmint

To prepare the herbs:

Combine all the herbs, if dried, and store them in an airtight container, away from the light.

To make the tea:

Measure 2 teaspoons of the tea mixture into a tea infuser or strainer and set it in a cup. Pour boiling water (not hot water from the tap) over the infuser and cover the cup with a saucer. Let the tea steep for 5 minutes. Remove the infuser and sweeten with honey if desired.

Yield: About 16 teaspoons, enough for 8 cups of tea

Don't Dry Herbs in the Microwave

Herbs dried in the microwave lose much of their flavor. If you've tried this method, you may have noticed a pleasant fragrance when you opened the microwave door. That was the oils that have been vaporized from the herbs. If the fragrance is in the air, it's not in the herbs!

Lemon Herb Muffins

Here's one of my favorite muffin recipes. The muffins freeze well, so they can be made ahead of time and then defrosted one at a time. To defrost, take a muffin from the freezer, wrap it loosely in plastic wrap, and microwave it for about 35 seconds.

I like my muffins to be heavy, so I always break the first rule of good cooking by not sifting the flour. If you want a lighter, cake-like muffin, go ahead and sift the flour as many times as you feel necessary.

Muffins

- 1 teaspoon fresh or dried lemon thyme leaves (use regular thyme if lemon isn't available)
- 1 teaspoon fresh or dried lemon balm leaves
- 1 tablespoon finely snipped fresh lemon-grass
- 1 teaspoon grated lemon peel
- 1 cup milk, scalded in microwave
- 1 cup butter-flavored vegetable shortening
- 2 cups sugar
- 5 eggs
- 3 cups self-rising flour, or 3 cups all-purpose flour and 2 teaspoons baking powder

Topping

- ¼ cup sugar
- ¼ cup instant lemonade mix

To make the muffins:

Preheat the oven to 350°F. Add the lemon thyme, lemon balm, lemongrass, and lemon peel to the hot milk and set aside to steep.

In the food processor, combine the shortening and sugar. Pulse for a few seconds. Add the eggs and blend briefly.

Pour the hot milk mixture into a blender and blend until most of the herb pieces are well chopped. Add to the food processor and blend. Add the flour and pulse briefly until completely mixed.

Spoon or pour the batter into greased muffin tins, filling each cup about two-thirds full. (You can use paper muffin liners if you wish. If so, it's not necessary to grease the cups.) Bake for about 15 minutes. Remove the muffins from the tins as soon as they can be handled.

To make the topping:

Combine the sugar and instant lemonade mix in a shallow dish. Using a pastry brush, brush the hot muffin tops lightly with water, then immediately dip in the topping. Set aside to cool before serving or freezing.

Yield: Makes approximately 1 dozen muffins

A Creative Retreat

Several very successful computer and electronics companies have realized that offering employees quiet places to meditate, conduct quiet discussions, or simply reflect on their work is one of the best investments they can make. They've found that having relaxing spaces available in the workplace results in happier workers, who produce more creative ideas.

I know of a production pottery company in the Ozarks that turns out hundreds of thousands of pottery and glass products a year and has some unusual elements in the work setting. The owners have created a park with pathways where employees can stroll, arbors and gazebos for quiet lunches, and a pond with frogs, birds, and fish. They also have an indoor pool, sauna, and hot tub for employees to use. One of the owners told me that she values the creativity of her workers, and the best way she can encourage that is to give them places to exchange ideas, rest, and restore their creative energy. "After all," she said, "my employees are my most important asset. When I invest in their creativity, they make money for me."

Another example that comes to mind is a book and magazine publishing company that provides a place for their employees to take naps in the afternoon. "Naps?" I asked. "Yes," the marketing supervisor told me. "If an employee is working on an idea for a book or editing an article, how good a job will they be doing if they are nodding off to sleep? A fifteen-minute nap is a good investment in productivity. We'd rather have a fully awake employee for most of the day than a partially awake employee for some of the day. Naps have been shown to keep mistakes to a minimum for us."

Nurturing Your Own Creativity

What if you are not a part of such an innovative corporate structure? What if it's just you and the kids, a job you don't really care much about, or a schedule that makes you a slave to everyone else's schedule? You don't have to wait for your employer to make an investment in your creative energy; you can do it yourself.

The Craftsman-style arbor (see page 81), featuring a bench on either side, may be the catalyst you need to establish your own backyard-stress reduction spot.

Invite one or two people to sit under the arbor you built. It isn't necessary to plan a discussion topic; you may just want to talk over what's going on in your lives, renew your friendship, or even gossip about the neighbors. One of my friends, whom I had neglected to contact regularly but felt warmly toward, told me that a friendship is like a plant. If you don't feed and water it and give it attention, it will die.

Nurture your friendships and renew yourself with some simple tea and cake in the garden. The following tea mixture can be made ahead of time and stored in an airtight jar in a reasonably dark place, such as the kitchen cabinet or pantry. (Light will destroy the color and flavor of the herbs quickly.)

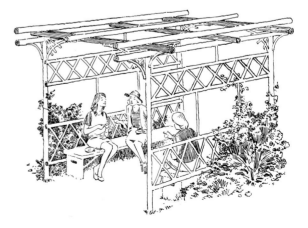

Black Tea and Rose Petals

1 cup dried rose petals (fragrant roses, especially red or deep pink, from shrub rose or old-rose varieties are best; be sure they have not been sprayed with insecticide)
½ cup good black tea leaves (choose a loose-leaf orange pekoe or similar unflavored black tea)

Combine the rose petals and tea leaves. Warm the teapot by filling it with hot tap water and allowing it to sit. Bring a pot of cold water to a boil. Put 2 teaspoons of tea for each cup in a tea infuser. Empty the teapot and put the infuser inside. Pour in as many cups of boiling water as you have tea for. Place the lid on the pot and let steep for 5 to 7 minutes.

Yield: 1½ cups, enough to make 25–30 cups

Mixed Berry Shortcake

Use fresh or frozen berries. This can be made several days ahead and refrigerated until you're ready to serve it.

1 recipe shortcake or 1 package yellow cake mix, baked in shallow pan
1 8-ounce package cream cheese, softened
1 3.4-ounce package French vanilla instant pudding mix
3 cups cold milk

2 tablespoons finely snipped fresh lemon verbena leaves
1 8-ounce container frozen whipped topping, thawed
1 cup red raspberries
1 cup black raspberries or blackberries
1 cup blueberries
½ cup cranberry juice
2 cups sugar
  pinch of ground coriander
2 tablespoons cornstarch dissolved in   cup cranberry juice

The day before you plan to serve the dessert, make the shortcake or yellow cake. When cool, store in an airtight container.

Several hours before serving the dessert, combine the cream cheese, pudding, milk, and lemon verbena in a food processor or a mixing bowl. Blend until smooth. Fold in the whipped topping. Chill completely.

Combine the berries and the ½ cup cranberry juice in a saucepan. Bring to a boil and add the sugar and coriander, stirring briefly. Quickly add the thoroughly mixed cornstarch–cranberry juice mixture and stir. Turn off the heat and continue stirring for a few seconds until the berries thicken. Set aside to cool.

Cut the shortcake into squares (or rounds if you have a biscuit cutter). Place each square on a dessert plate and top with berries. Add a spoonful of topping. Serve extra topping on the side. The topping will keep for up to a week in the refrigerator and is good on any fruit dish, such as strawberry shortcake or pancakes with fruit.

Yield: About 8 servings

A Backyard Garden Party

Over the years, people have sent me photos of the ways they have used their own versions of my trellis designs as backdrops for special events in their lives. One family sent photos of a young daughter's garden tea parties. The old rustic bentwood, covered with scarlet runner bean blossoms, made a lovely picture with the child-sized table and chairs and little girls sipping afternoon tea with their dolls.

Another photo shows a wedding in front of a large bentwood trellis in the family's garden. The trellis stands in front of a large bed of roses, with one yellow climbing rose trained up the trellis. At the base are baskets of flowers. The bride and groom are shown surrounded by candles, flowers, and friends. The curving lines of the trellis, covered with vines and flowers, give the wedding photos a timeless quality of strength and stability.

Recipes for Entertaining a Crowd

Following are some of my favorite recipes for entertaining large groups of people. I like to use recipes like these that freeze well and can be expanded easily. If you make the recipe ahead of time and freeze it, you will be relaxed and ready to entertain.

Ruby Red Herbal Punch

I've made this drink for as many as 150 people. Much of the preparation is done in advance, with the ingredients being combined in a punch bowl just before the guests are to be served. I nearly always get requests for the recipe from the guests. Sometimes I call this recipe the tea for people who don't like herbal tea. Even teenagers, who are pretty persnickety about their beverages, give good reviews and come back for seconds.

    12 cups water
     2 lemons, thinly sliced
     5 fresh lemongrass leaves, or 2 table-
        spoons dried
     2 cups fresh lemon balm leaves and stems
     3 quart-sized iced tea bags
     4 red or pink hibiscus flowers, petals only
     2 cups honey or sugar
     1 gallon cran-raspberry juice, chilled
     1 cup grenadine (pomegranate juice)
     2 quarts ginger ale, chilled
        edible flowers or lemon slices for gar-
        nish (optional)

Bring the water to a boil in a large pot. Add the lemon slices and lemongrass and simmer for 5 minutes. Turn off the heat and add the lemon balm, tea bags, and hibiscus flowers. Let steep 3 to 4 hours, until cool. Strain and chill. Add honey or sugar.

Divide the liquid and freeze one portion in freezer containers. Chill the punch bowl in the freezer or refrigerator. Refrigerate remaining liquid.

To serve, put the frozen liquid in the punch bowl, add the juice and grenadine, and part of the chilled liquid. Pour in the ginger ale at the very end. If desired, add edible flowers or fresh lemon slices to the bowl for garnish. Freeze any leftover punch for later use.

Yield: *Serves approx. 25 people*

Lemon Balm Blueberry Cake

I like the fresh flavor of lemony herbs in summer and am always concocting new ways to use them with seasonal fruits and flowers. During the 7 years that I hosted an herb festival at my farm, I developed many cake recipes that combined several lemon-flavored herbs. Here is one of my favorites, which combines the flavor of the herbs with fresh or frozen blueberries.

Cake
    ¾ cup milk
     2 tablespoons fresh lemon balm leaves,
        stems removed
     1 tablespoon finely snipped fresh lemon-
        grass
     1 teaspoon fresh lemon thyme leaves (use
        regular thyme if lemon isn't available)

        6 tablespoons butter, softened
        1 cup sugar
        2 eggs
        2 cups all-purpose flour
    1 ½ teaspoons baking powder
        ¼ teaspoon salt
        1 tablespoon grated lemon peel
        2 cups fresh or frozen blueberries

To make the cake:

Preheat the oven to 350°F. Heat the milk to boiling in the microwave. Put the hot milk and herbs in a blender and mix well. Set aside to steep.

In a large bowl, cream the butter and sugar. Add the eggs and beat briefly. Stir in the flour, baking powder, and salt. Then add the lemon peel and hot milk-herb mixture and mix well. Add blueberries, stirring just enough to combine. Pour into a greased 9 × 5-inch bread pan and bake for about 50 minutes. Test for doneness. If the tester comes out with batter on it, continue baking for a few minutes more. Let cool slightly, then remove from the pan.

Rose Petal Topping

    1 ½ cups hot water
        2 cups rose petals (fragrant roses, especially red or deep pink, from shrub rose or old-rose varieties are best; be sure they have not been sprayed with insecticide)
        2 cups sugar
        1 teaspoon fresh lemon juice
        red food coloring (optional)
        fresh rose petals for garnish

To make the topping:

In a saucepan, combine the water and rose petals. Bring to boil, reduce the heat, and simmer for about 5 minutes, until the color is gone from the petals. Strain. Return to the heat and add the sugar and lemon juice. Simmer slowly, stirring until the sugar is dissolved. Remove from the heat and cool. Add a few drops of red food color if desired. Refrigerate until ready to use.

To serve the cake, cut it into slices and place on dessert plates. Pour a small amount of topping over each slice. Sprinkle with fresh rose petals.

Yield: Serves 8–10 people

A Place to Celebrate the Fruits of the Earth

Standing over a rustic wooden gate leading into my garden is a large arbor laden with wild grapevines. The vines are a reminder of a jelly-making session years ago when I gathered about a bushel of especially tasty wild grapes along the rural road to my farm and boiled the fruit for jelly. Once the juice was pressed out, I discarded the seeds, stems, and skins. The following year, the seeds sprouted in the compost pit, and I transplanted a couple to an old cedar arbor. This arbor, built a decade ago of previously used cedar poles, finally collapsed under the weight of the grapes, and I replaced it with the present structure.

The grapes have grown substantial trunks in 10 years, even though I annually prune back the long runners. One corner of the arbor has red honeysuckle, while another shady corner plays host to Dutchman's-pipe. Moonvines are planted every spring on two of the posts. Although it may not be the best practice to plant so many vines on one arbor, the effect is pleasing.

The moonvine blossoms open at night, lending their delightful fragrance to the evening air. In spring, the grape blossoms give off a pleasant aroma. All summer long, the arbor is a cool and shady spot. I keep an old oak love seat, kind of a rocker-built-for-two, in the shade of the vines. There is ample room for eight or more chairs in the arbor, and I've hosted several small groups there.

Black Tea with Chamomile

Here's a tea I've served many times under this arbor. The chamomile gives a pleasant apple flavor and aroma that mixes well with the other ingredients. This tea is tasty in summer and winter.

1 **tea bag good-quality black tea or 1 tablespoon loose black tea**
2 **teaspoons dried chamomile**
2 **teaspoons fresh or dried rose hips**
4 **cups boiling water**
3 **tablespoons orange juice concentrate honey (optional)**

Put the tea, chamomile, and rose hips in a container with a cover (or in a teapot) and pour the boiling water over all. Cover and let steep for 7 minutes. Stir in the orange juice and serve over ice. Sweeten with honey, if desired.

Variation:

In winter, add 2 whole cloves and a tiny piece of cinnamon stick to the herbs. Let steep, then serve hot.

Observing the Seasons

You can enjoy your bentwood creations in any season. Sometimes I take a cup of hot tea and a slice of freshly baked bread outdoors in winter. I have a special bench in the garden that I like, and I dust off the snow and have a winter picnic there. The garden is so quiet in winter. Many of the herbs are hidden away, but thyme and sage stay green all season, contrasting beautifully with the white snow. My cat usually comes along, and together we watch the winter birds as they scratch for their lunches. It is comforting to know that the flowers and plants rest, too, sleeping under the soft snow, their work on hold until a warmer time.

It takes some practice to use the garden for relaxing if you aren't used to it. You may find it easier to sit indoors instead of being outside. But with some practice, you can get accustomed to spending a few minutes, or a few hours, in the garden. Any quiet place will do. The important thing is to take the time to slow down, renew your energy, and reflect on the beauty around you. I hope your bentwood structures will help you see the wonders of nature more clearly, and often.

Resources

In visiting with the people listed below, each said essentially the same thing: if you can find green wood for making trellises in your local area, that is the best option. But if you can't find wood locally, having exhausted all the possibilities in chapter 1, you might want to check with the sources listed below that offer cuttings. Some will ship green limbs for trellis uprights. Others suggest that you might want to order cuttings to grow your own wood. All of these sources may be willing to help crafters locate materials.

Organizations

American Willow Growers Network
Bonnie Gale
412 Country Road 31
Norwich, NY 13815
(607) 336-9031
This is a network of people dedicated to developing the potential of willows by exchanging cuttings and information. It is primarily focused on basketry. Network membership includes the possibility of ordering a wide assortment of inexpensive willow cuttings for growing. The newsletter lists sources for basketry supplies, willow cuttings, and willow craft and basket-weaving information. Bonnie Gale also offers dried willow to soak for crafts, small trellises, or baskets. It is available in 3- to 8-foot lengths in a variety of colors. Write for her English Basketry Willows catalog at this address.

Bentwood Trellis Workshops

Jim Long
Long Creek Herbs
P.O. Box 127
Blue Eye, MO 65611
(417) 779-5450
www.LongCreekHerbs.com
Trellis-making workshops for your club or organization, at your location by advance reservation. A catalog of books and herb products is available for $2, refundable with order.

Chris Spindler
Peconic River Herb Farm
310-C River Road
Calverton, NY 11933
(516) 369-0058
Trellis-making classes, apprenticeships, and workshops at Peconic River Herb Farm throughout the summer months. Write for a calendar of classes.

Sources of Wood and Cuttings

Bear Creek Nursery
Box 411
Northport, WA 99157
(509) 732-4417
Suppliers of nursery stock cuttings, including several varieties of willow, for growing. Catalog on request.

Willowglen Nursery
Lee Zieke Lee
3512 Lost Mile Road
Decorah, IA 52101
(319) 735-5570
Can supply willow stakes and poles, as well as cuttings for growing. Occasionally offers classes.

Other Storey Titles You Will Enjoy

Garden Retreats, by David and Jeanie Stiles. Garden structures, from simple benches to elegant gazebos, can provide the focal points for relaxing garden retreats. Here are step-by-step instructions for 22 garden carpentry projects. 160 pages. Paperback. ISBN 1-58017-149-4.

Making Bent Willow Furniture, by Brenda and Brian Cameron. A companion volume in The Rustic Home Series. A step-by-step illustrated guide to the traditional craft of making bent willow furniture. Includes both beginning and advanced projects, from mirror frames to love seats to double-bed headboards, as well as reference charts and tips for finding, identifying, and harvesting different types of willow. 144 pages. Includes 16 pages of full-color photographs. Paperback. ISBN 1-58017-048-X.

Rustic Retreats: A Build-It-Yourself Guide, by David and Jeanie Stiles. A step-by-step illustrated guide to building a wide variety of both temporary and permanent backyard and woodland structures. Projects include basic lean-tos, tree houses, a pergola for outdoor dining, a garden pavilion, a cordwood cabin, a yurt, a sauna "hut," and more. Also features a beginning section on basic building techniques, essential tools, safety tips, as well as instructions for flooring (wooden or brick), various kinds of roofs, windows, and doors, and even a few wind sculptures for your special retreat. 160 pages. Paperback. ISBN 1-58017-035-8.

The Feng Shui Garden: Design Your Garden for Health, Wealth, and Happiness, by Gill Hale. A fascinating exploration of gardening in accordance with Feng Shui principles. Teaches readers how to create balanced outdoor spaces that positively influence health, relationships, and happiness. Features illustrated garden plans, including window boxes, terraces, and rooftop gardens, plus garden paths, statuary, and outbuildings. 128 pages. Full-color photographs and illustrations. Paperback. ISBN 1-58017-022-6.

Stonework: Techniques and Projects, by Charles McRaven. This complete guide includes fully illustrated, step-by-step instructions for 22 attractive projects, including walls, porches, pools, seats, waterfalls, and even a bridge. Advice on gathering and handling stone and hiring stonemasons is also included. 192 pages. Paperback. ISBN 0-88266-976-1.

Stonescaping: A Guide to Using Stone in Your Garden, by Jan Whitner. A thorough guide to incorporating stone into many garden features, including paths, steps, walls, ponds, and rock gardens. More than 20 designs are included. 168 pages. Paperback. ISBN 0-88266-755-6.

These and other books from Storey Publishing are available wherever quality books are sold or by calling 1-800-441-5700. Visit us at www.storey.com.